D1165402

TSUNAMIS

TSUNAMIS

Other books in the Great Disasters series:

TSUNAMIS

Nancy Harris, *Book Editor*

Daniel Leone, *President*
Bonnie Szumski, *Publisher*
Scott Barbour, *Managing Editor*

THOMSON

GALE

San Diego • Detroit • New York • San Francisco • Cleveland
New Haven, Conn. • Waterville, Maine • London • Munich

For more information, contact
Greenhaven Press
27500 Drake Rd.
Farmington Hills, MI 48331-3535
Or you can visit our Internet site at http://www.gale.com

Cover credit: © Associated Press, AP
AP/Wide World Photos, 51, 76
FEMA, 68
NOAA Central Library, 14

LIBRARY OF CONGRESS CATALOGING-IN-PUBLICATION DATA

Tsunamis / Nancy Harris, book editor.
    p. cm. — (Great disasters)
Includes bibliographical references and index.
ISBN 0-7377-1877-3 (pbk. : alk. paper) —
ISBN 0-7377-1876-5 (lib. bdg. : alk. paper)
    1. Tsunamis. 2. Natural disasters. I. Harris, Nancy. II. Great disasters (Greenhaven Press)
GC221.2.T74 2003
551.47'024—dc21   2003040859

CONTENTS

Chapter 2: Tsunami Disasters

communities for future tsunamis and to promote scientific research and understanding of tsunamis.

Humans have an ambivalent relationship with their home planet, nurtured on the one hand by Earth's bounty but devastated on the other hand by its catastrophic natural disasters. While these events are the results of the natural processes of Earth, their consequences for humans frequently include the disastrous destruction of lives and property. For example, when the volcanic island of Krakatau exploded in 1883, the eruption generated vast seismic sea waves called tsunamis that killed about thirty-six thousand people in Indonesia. In a single twenty-four-hour period in the United States in 1974, at least 148 tornadoes carved paths of death and destruction across thirteen states. In 1976, an earthquake completely destroyed the industrial city of Tangshan, China, killing more than 250,000 residents.

Some natural disasters have gone beyond relatively localized destruction to completely alter the course of human history. Archaeological evidence suggests that one of the greatest natural disasters in world history happened in A.D. 535, when an Indonesian "supervolcano" exploded near the same site where Krakatau arose later. The dust and debris from this gigantic eruption blocked the light and heat of the sun for eighteen months, radically altering weather patterns around the world and causing crop failure in Asia and the Middle East. Rodent populations increased with the weather changes, causing an epidemic of bubonic plague that decimated entire populations in Africa and Europe. The most powerful volcanic eruption in recorded human history also happened in Indonesia. When the volcano Tambora erupted in 1815, it ejected an estimated 1.7 million tons of debris in an explosion that was heard more than a thousand miles away and that continued to rumble for three months. Atmospheric dust from the eruption blocked much of the sun's heat, producing what was called "the year without summer" and creating worldwide climatic havoc, starvation, and disease.

As these examples illustrate, natural disasters can have as much impact on human societies as the bloodiest wars and most chaotic political revolutions. Therefore, they are as worthy of study as the major events of world history. As with the study of social and political events, the exploration of natural disasters can illuminate the causes of these catastrophes and target the lessons learned about how to mitigate and prevent the loss of life when disaster strikes again. By examining these events and the forces behind them, the Greenhaven Press Great Disasters series is designed to help students better understand such cataclysmic events. Each anthology in the series focuses on a specific type of natural disaster or a particular disastrous event in history. An introductory essay provides a general overview of the subject of the anthology, placing natural disasters in historical and scientific context. The essays that follow, written by specialists in the field, researchers, journalists, witnesses, and scientists, explore the science and nature of natural disasters, describing particular disasters in detail and discussing related issues, such as predicting, averting, or managing disasters. To aid the reader in choosing appropriate material, each essay is preceded by a concise summary of its content and biographical information about its author.

In addition, each volume contains extensive material to help the student researcher. An annotated table of contents and a comprehensive index help readers quickly locate particular subjects of interest. To guide students in further research, each volume features an extensive bibliography including books, periodicals, and related Internet websites. Finally, appendixes provide glossaries of terms, tables of measurements, chronological charts of major disasters, and related materials. With its many useful features, the Greenhaven Press Great Disasters series offers students a fascinating and awe-inspiring look at the deadly power of Earth's natural forces and their catastrophic impact on humans.

INTRODUCTION

On August 27, 1883, a volcano on the Indonesian island of Krakatau exploded, collapsing eleven square miles of the island's surface and creating sound waves that could be heard three thousand miles away. Tsunami waves generated by the eruption were powerful enough to rip six hundred-pound blocks of coral from the sea bottom and deposit them onshore. Mountainous walls of water swamped a nearby seaside village, killing all but one of its twenty-seven hundred inhabitants, and waves climbed the hill behind the village to an estimated height of 130 feet, razing the houses there. These tsunamis were responsible for the destruction of 165 settlements in the area and for the deaths of almost thirty-six thousand people.

A more recent tsunami disaster occurred on the Pacific island country of Papua New Guinea in 1998. Residents of Papua New Guinea, a nation of 4 million people, were beginning the celebration of a four-day national holiday when an earthquake shook the area. Scientists believe that an underwater landslide generated by the earthquake produced three gigantic tsunami waves. Villagers in the path of the tsunamis reported hearing sounds like jet fighters approaching as monstrous waves surged toward their villages. Tsunami waves crashed ashore and flooded a twenty-mile stretch of beach, completely washing away two villages and flooding many others. Officials estimated that three thousand people were killed or missing and another five thousand were left homeless by the disaster. Adding to the tragedy was the fact that many schoolchildren were home for the holidays and away from the safer ground of their inland schools. As a result, the tsunami killed almost an entire generation of children and is considered one of the worst disasters to strike Papua New Guinea in its history.

These events illustrate the destructive potential of tsunamis, which are the largest, rarest, and most powerful waves in the world. In their paths, buildings are easily crushed, trees are snapped in half, and ships are smashed against cliffs or carried far inland and beached.

Harbor Waves

Tsunami is a Japanese word meaning "harbor wave." Tsunamis are also known as seismic sea waves. In the past, they were mistakenly referred to as "tidal waves," but they have nothing to do with the tides. A tsunami is a wave, or usually a series of waves, that is triggered by any event that suddenly causes a large disruption in the sea level. Although the majority of these triggering events are earthquakes, submarine volcanoes, and landslides, asteroid or meteorite impacts can also generate tsunamis. These events produce a sudden disturbance in the seafloor, which causes the seafloor to either uplift or drop and creates a displacement in the water directly above it. This water displacement is the birth of a tsunami, which becomes a series of fast-moving, low, long waves that radiate outward in all directions like ripples in a pond. Tsunamis are often generated in relatively deep water, and then they travel through shallow water to strike shore. Many pass through varying depths and over complex seafloor topography, causing the waves to continuously evolve and change shape so that a tsunami generated from an earthquake off the coast of Chile may look entirely different on the Chilean coast than when it strikes later on a Hawaiian beach.

Tsunamis travel through the open sea at speeds between three hundred to six hundred miles per hour, a speed within the cruising range of a Boeing 747, and their wave crests can be as long as 300 miles. Despite their monstrous size, tsunamis can go unnoticed in the open sea because, although their depth may be over one thousand feet, their height can be less than three feet at sea. In addition, the distance between their wave crests may be 60 to 120 miles, giving the tsunamis very gentle slopes and allowing them to pass practically unnoticed by ships or aircraft.

As tsunami waves hit shallow water near coastlines, in harbors, or in narrow inlets, they drag bottom and their speed diminishes rapidly. All their tremendous forward-moving energy is then transferred into the buildup of huge waves with enormously magnified heights. When these monstrous waves reach the shore, they do not break and retreat like regular wind-generated waves. Instead, they advance as a massive wall of water that can travel as far as twelve miles inland. These powerful waves can travel all the way across the Pacific Ocean, where over 90 percent of tsunamis occur. The great 1960 Chilean earthquake produced tsunamis that traveled over five thousand miles to strike Hilo, Hawaii, caus-

Tsunamis can travel up to twelve miles inland, decimating coastal towns. These Alaskan fishing boats were washed ashore by a tsunami in 1963.

ing more than $20 million in property damage and 61 deaths. Then the waves continued an additional five thousand miles to cause considerable damage along the coast of Japan, where 180 people were reported killed or missing. Still not exhausted, the tsunamis killed 20 more people in the Philippines and damaged coastal areas of New Zealand. Several days afterward, tidal gauges in Hilo registered wave activity as the tsunamis continued to bounce around the Pacific basin. Although these are impressive wave behaviors creating dramatic effects, tsunami events are relatively rare, with damaging tsunamis striking somewhere in the world only once per year and the most disastrous tsunamis occuring only once every ten years.

Prediction and Preparedness

Although scientists know much about how tsunamis form, travel, and strike the shore, and they employ state-of-the-art computer tsunami simulations to help in their research, more information is necessary to improve prediction times and to prevent disasters. Tsunami historic records are short and incomplete, making it difficult to predict the probability of a tsunami strike, and scientists have done relatively little research on the seafloor, an important area in tsunami research. Questions continue to baffle seismologists and oceanographers, such as why relatively small earthquakes generate very large tsunamis or why some tsunamis inexplicably diminish to little more than a high tide before striking the shore.

Tsunami disasters have prompted scientists and others to develop programs such as the International Tsunami Warning System (ITWS), created in 1965. This program has twenty-five participating member countries throughout the Pacific Ocean area, which communicate with each other in the event of a possible tsunami threat. The development of new sensors, called bottom-pressure recorders, has aided the tsunami warning system effort. These sensors detect the presence of a tsunami more accurately than previous measuring techniques, and some scientists believe that the sensors may be the best hope for better and more reliable early tsunami warnings.

Reliable tsunami warnings are useless if those in danger are not educated about tsunamis. People living, working, and playing along the shore need to know how to recognize the warning signs of an approaching tsunami, which can include ground shaking, a loud banging noise, a rapid drop in sea level, or a retreat of water from the shoreline. The public should also know that a tsunami threat may continue for a long time after the initial wave has hit because it may be hours before the second or third wave crashes. In the past, people have lost their lives by prematurely returning to an area and being surprised and engulfed by later waves. Because of this wave behavior, search-and-rescue personnel have difficulty planning their procedures, making advanced planning and education vital in areas where tsunamis threaten. To help with advance planning and education, geologists have created inundation (flood) maps to show which coastal areas are at the highest risk for tsunamis. Local communities can educate themselves about tsunami risks by using these maps, and emergency personnel can use the maps to plan their operations in the event of a tsunami. In Hawaii, inundation maps are printed in telephone books, and more map distribution is planned for the U.S. Pacific coast.

Like volcanoes, earthquakes, and other natural disasters, tsunamis cannot be prevented, but maps, more sophisticated warning systems, and public education and preparedness programs can help to lessen the destructive impact of these awesome waves.

The Science and Study of Tsunamis

The Nature and Characteristics of Tsunamis

BY JAMES F. LANDER AND PATRICIA A. LOCKRIDGE

Tsunamis, or seismic sea waves, are somewhat rare events but have been responsible for hundreds of deaths and millions of dollars worth of property damage in the United States and its territories. In the following selection, James F. Lander and Patricia A. Lockridge explain that these waves, sometimes incorrectly called "tidal waves," are usually caused when a large mass of earth on the bottom of the ocean drops or rises and displaces a column of water above it. The displaced water forms a large wave or series of waves that can travel hundreds of miles across the ocean. Tsunamis can reach speeds higher than 620 miles per hour. They can go unnoticed in deep water, where they appear to be only a few feet high and their wavelengths, the distance from one wave crest to another, can be hundreds of miles apart. However, as the waves reach shallow water, where they are slowed, their heights can increase to one hundred feet. Major tsunamis occur mainly in the Pacific Ocean, where oceanic tectonic plates collide with, and dip below, continental plates, causing many of the earth's earthquakes. Lander is the former deputy director of the National Geophysical Data Center. Lockridge maintains the historical tsunami database at the center.

"Tsunami" is a Japanese word meaning "harbor wave." It is a water wave or a series of waves generated by an impulsive vertical displacement of the surface of the ocean or other body of water. Other terms for "tsunami" found in the literature include: seismic sea wave, Flutwellen, vloedgolven, raz de marée, vagues sismique, maremoto, and, in-

James F. Lander and Patricia A. Lockridge, *United States Tsunamis: 1690–1988.* Washington, DC: U.S. Department of Commerce, August 1989.

correctly, tidal wave. The term "tidal wave" is frequently used in the older literature and in popular accounts, but is now considered incorrect. Tides are produced by the gravitational attraction of the sun and moon and occur predictably with twelve hour periods. The effects of a tsunami may be increased or decreased depending on the level of the tide, but otherwise the two phenomena are independent.

Although there are warning systems for tsunamis occurring around the Pacific, including local and regional warning systems in Hawaii and Alaska, the risks from future tsunamis are still not fully known. Some events, such as that in Prince William Sound, Alaska, in March 1964, can be devastating over large distances. Even over short distances along a coast, the heights of a tsunami wave will vary considerably. An important part of the risk assessment is to gain a clearer understanding of the effects of past tsunamis.

Where Tsunamis Occur

Tsunamis have been reported since ancient times. They have been documented extensively, especially in Japan and the Mediterranean areas. The first recorded tsunami occurred off the coast of Syria in 2000 B.C. Since 1900 (the beginning of instrumentally located earthquakes), most tsunamis have been generated in Japan, Peru, Chile, New Guinea, and the Solomon Islands. However, the only regions that have generated remote-source tsunamis affecting the entire Pacific Basin are the Kamchatka Peninsula, the Aleutian Islands, the Gulf of Alaska, and the coast of South America. Hawaii, because of its location in the center of the Pacific Basin, has experienced tsunamis generated in all parts of the Pacific.

The Mediterranean and Caribbean Seas both have small subduction zones, and have histories of locally destructive tsunamis. Only a few tsunamis have been generated in the Atlantic and Indian Oceans. In the Atlantic Ocean, there are no subduction zones at the edges of plate boundaries to spawn such waves except small subduction zones under the Caribbean and Scotia arcs. In the Indian Ocean, however, the Indo-Australian plate is being subducted beneath the Eurasian plate at its east margin. Therefore, most tsunamis generated in this area are propagated toward the southwest shores of Java and Sumatra, rather than into the Indian Ocean.

Causes of Tsunamis

Most tsunamis are caused by a rapid vertical movement along a break in the Earth's crust (i.e., their origin is tectonic). A tsunami is generated when a large mass of earth on the bottom of the ocean drops or rises, thereby displacing the column of water directly above it. This type of displacement commonly occurs in large subduction zones, where the collision of two tectonic plates causes the oceanic plate to dip beneath the continental plate to form deep ocean trenches. Most shallow earthquakes occur offshore in these trenches.

Subduction occurs along most of the island arcs and coastal areas of the Pacific, the notable exception being the west coast of the United States and Canada. Movement along the faults there is largely strike–slip, having little vertical displacement, and the movement produces few local tsunamis.

Volcanoes have generated significant tsunamis with death tolls as large as 30,000 people from a single event. Roughly one-fourth of the deaths occurring during volcanic eruptions where tsunamis were generated, were the result of the tsunami rather than the volcano. A tsunami is an effective transmitter of energy to areas outside the reach of the volcanic eruption itself. The most efficient methods of tsunami generation by volcanoes include disruption of a body of water by the collapse of all or part

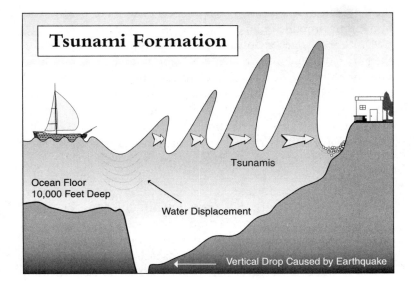

Tsunami Formation

Tsunamis

Ocean Floor
10,000 Feet Deep

Water Displacement

Vertical Drop Caused by Earthquake

of the volcanic edifice, subsidence, an explosion, a landslide, a glowing avalanche, and an earthquake accompanying or preceding the eruption. Roughly one-half of all volcanic tsunamis are generated at calderas or at cones within calderas. Submarine eruptions may also cause minor tsunamis.

Locally destructive tsunamis may be generated by subaerial and submarine landslides into bays or lakes. Lituya Bay, Alaska, has been the site of several landslide-generated tsunamis, including one in 1958 that produced a splash wave that removed trees to a height of 525 m. It also caused a tsunami of at least 50 m in the bay. The 1964 Prince William Sound earthquake triggered at least four submarine landslides, which accounted for 71 to 82 of the 106 fatalities in Alaska for the 1964 event. However, it is tectonic earthquake–generated tsunamis (those produced by a major deformation of Earth's crust) that may affect the entire Pacific Basin.

Other possible but less efficient methods of tsunami generation include: strong oscillations of the bottom of the ocean, or transmission of energy to a column of water from a seismic impulse (e.g., a deep-focus earthquake that has no surface rupture); transmission of energy from a horizontal seismic impulse to the water column through a vertical or inclined wall such as a bathymetric ridge; strong turbidity currents; underwater and abovewater explosions. Several mechanisms commonly are involved in the generation of a tsunami (e.g., vertical movement of the crust by a seismic impulse or an earthquake, and a submarine landslide).

Our knowledge of tsunami generation is incomplete, because the generation phenomena has not been observed nor measured directly. However, studies of tsunami data suggest that the size of a tsunami is directly related to: the size of the shallow-focus earthquake, the area and shape of the rupture zone, the rate of displacement and sense of motion of the ocean-floor in the source (epicentral) area, the amount of displacement of the rupture zone, and the depth of the water in the source area.

It is also observed that long-period tsunamis are generated by large-magnitude earthquakes associated with seafloor deformation of the continental shelf; while, shorter period tsunamis are generated by smaller magnitude earthquakes associated with seafloor deformation in deeper water beyond the continental shelf.

Once the energy from an undersea disturbance has been transmitted to the column of water, the wave can propagate outward

from the source at a speed of more than 1,000 km per hour depending on the depth of the water. Because the height of the
long-period waves in the open ocean is commonly 1 m or less
and their wavelength is hundreds of kilometers, they pass unnoticed by observers in ships or planes in the region. As the tsunami
enters shallow water along coastlines, the velocity of its waves is
reduced, and the height of each wave increases. The waves pile
up on shore especially in the region of the earthquake source,
producing a "local tsunami." Some dramatic examples of such
local tsunamis include those generated by landslides or by volcanic eruptions, which have caused "runup" heights of 30 to 50
m in some coastal areas.

The Atlantic Megatsunami

By Edwin Unsworth

A British scientific study suggests that the east coast of the United States is destined to be inundated by a huge tsunami, or "megatsunami." In the following excerpt, Edwin Unsworth reports that the megatsunami will be caused by a massive landslide collapsing from the side of a volcano located in the Canary Islands off the west coast of Africa. This landslide could create a wave 2,145 feet tall that would travel across the Atlantic Ocean at about 450 miles per hour, threatening the cities of Miami, Boston, and New York. Edwin Unsworth is a writer for Business Insurance, *a weekly publication that covers news on insurance topics.*

I t may not happen today, or even tomorrow, but the entire East Coast of the United States is destined one day to be inundated by a mega-tsunami, according to a scientific study. Bill McGuire, a scientist from the Benfield Greig Hazard Research Centre at University College, London, which has been carrying out research since 1994, predicts that such a mega-tsunami "would be the biggest natural catastrophe in history." It will be caused by a landslide on the west flank of the Cumbre Vieja volcano on the island of La Palma, in the Canary Islands, off the west coast of Africa. "It's not a question of if (this will happen); it's a question of when," Mr. McGuire said. Simon Day, another scientist from the center, said that if the volcano's already-unstable west flank were to collapse in one block, almost 124 cubic miles of rock—equivalent to the land area of Toronto—would drop into the sea. The rock would fall into water 3.75 miles deep and create a wave 2,145 feet tall. That wave, which would travel across the Atlantic Ocean at about 450 mph, would weaken only slightly during its eight-hour transit; it is probable the wave would

Edwin Unsworth, "Atlantic Tsunami Risk Studied," *Business Insurance*, vol. 34, October 23, 2000, p. 59. Copyright © 2000 by Crain Communications, Inc. Reproduced by permission.

still be 130 to 165 feet high by the time it made landfall. The surge would create havoc as much as 12 miles inland, the scientists predict. The scientists made most of their comments in a BBC television documentary but they have been so concerned by their findings about the threat of mega-tsunamis, in general, that they have sent a warning letter to the British government. Chris Wilson, honorary secretary of the Geological Society, wrote to U.K. Science Minister Lord Sainsbury, warning him that the United Kingdom could be severely endangered by mega-tsunamis caused by the collapse of volcanic islands in the Atlantic. Mr. Wilson urged the setting up of a task force to look at a broad band of terrestrial disasters, including earthquakes and volcanoes.

Mega-Tsunamis Caused by Landslides

Whereas most tsunamis, or giant sea waves, are formed by underwater earthquakes, the biggest waves, known as mega-tsunamis, occur less often and are caused by large-scale landslides of the flanks of oceanic islands. The biggest tsunami caused by an earthquake is usually no more than 33 feet high. A collapse of the Hawaiian volcano, Kilauea, around 100,000 years ago, generated a series of waves that started out almost 1,320 feet high and were still over 66 feet high when they hit eastern Australia twelve hours later, scientists say. A much more recent example occurred in Lituya Bay, Alaska, on July 9, 1958. A gigantic landslide fell into the head of the bay, creating a huge splash and a wave that stripped timber and soil off the hillsides surrounding the bay to a height of 1,716 feet. The volcanoes of the Canary Islands have experienced major landslides in the past. The scientists say 1,000-ton limestone boulders recently discovered in the Bahamas may be the result of prehistoric tsunamis that had their source in the Canary Islands. Mr. Day, who began mapping La Palma in 1994, said an eruption of the ridge-shaped Cumbre Vieja in 1949 and resulting earthquakes caused the west side of the volcano to slide about 13 feet downward toward the sea, opening a fissure that stretches about one and one-quarter miles along the summit. By mapping volcanic vents formed by eruptions over hundreds of thousands of years along the north-south ridge of the volcano, Mr. Day concluded that the fault could be as much as 12 miles long, dissecting the entire length of the volcano. This means that a volcanic eruption could cause an entire side of Cumbre Vieja, a half-trillion tons of rock, to fall into the sea. Water within the rock is also contributing to the treacherous situation. When heated by a volcanic eruption, the water expands, adding to the pressure widening the fissure and pushing the land into the sea.

When the Earthquake Will Erupt

Mr. Day noted that global warming may be adding to the pressure and hastening the date of collapse. According to Mr. Day, there is no way to know when Cumbre Vieja will next erupt. He said, though, that there have been eruptions in 1646, 1712 and 1949, making it look as though an eruption occurs every two centuries or so. "So, it's likely that sometime during the next century, there'll be another eruption . . . but it'll be pretty soon in geological terms," he said. Mr. McGuire also pointed out that while the western flank could collapse with the next eruption of the Cumbre Vieja, it may take numerous eruptions to shake it loose. "We simply don't know. But, put it this way: if I was living in Miami or New York and I heard that the Cumbre Vieja was erupting, I'd be keeping a very close eye on the news," he said. Mr. Day said the areas most at risk include cities such as Miami, parts of Boston, and the coastal sections of New York suburbs. He said that the eight hours it would take the wave to travel to North America is "just enough time to get the message out to warn people. . . . But unless evacuation plans were incredibly efficient, it would not be enough time to get everybody out of the affected areas."

Chile and Peru: A Major Tsunami Zone

BY MICHAEL J. MOONEY

In the following selection, Michael J. Mooney explains that Chile and Peru experience more earthquakes and volcanic eruptions per square mile than any other part of the world; Chile alone reported 40 percent of all damaging tsunamis in the world during the twentieth century. Situated along the Pacific coast of South America, where one tectonic plate grinds under another, Chile and Peru are the most unstable areas in the seismic zone circling the Pacific Ocean. Earthquakes in this area generate massive seismic sea waves that sometimes cross the Pacific to damage Hawaii and Japan, where populations have ignored tsunami warnings, believing the distance made them safe. For this tsunami-prone area, scientists have developed a sophisticated warning system called Project THRUST (Tsunami Hazards Reduction Utilizing Systems Technology), which uses satellite communication to provide a speedy two-minute tsunami response time. Mooney is a freelance writer and photographer focusing on issues concerning the environment and natural phenomena.

On Thursday, August 13, 1868, two great earthquakes with magnitudes of 8.5 shook hundreds of miles of coast line in the "Big Bend" territory where Peru and Chile meet. These unprecedented shocks spawned the greatest seismic sea waves ever to strike South America's long, earthquake-prone Pacific coast.

Caught in the harbor of the Peruvian (now-Chilean) city of Arica was the U.S.S. *Wateree*, a Navy Civil War side-wheeler. Unable to escape to sea, the 205-foot iron gunboat and her crew

Michael J. Mooney, "Tsunami: When the Sea Quakes," *Americas*, vol. 42, 1990, pp. 24–29. Copyright © 1990 by *Americas*. Reproduced by permission.

were lifted atop a foaming 70-foot wave crest for their last—and strangest—voyage. According to an eyewitness, the *Wateree* was swept "completely over the town, scraping the tops of some of the buildings." The wave finally deposited the flat-bottomed *Wateree* and her crew, shaken but upright and intact, among the sand dunes a quarter of a mile inland.

Getting the ship back to sea was impossible, but the beached vessel nevertheless remained in commission for several months. During that extraordinary time ashore, the crew had to alter their procedures to suit the unique conditions. Roger Clancy describes how the captain "went ashore":

> The boatswain's mate piped the proper call and shouted the orders to have the captain's gig made ready to depart. Then there was a slight modification of normal shipboard routine. A seaman went overboard on a boom, slid down a line, and "unmoored" a burro. Then he rode away.

How Tsunami Are Formed

In the unending battle of tectonic titans, the giant Nazca Plate, submerged in the Pacific Ocean, grinds in implacably under the equally formidable South American Plate, forcing up the latter. This upward thrust, which created the Andes themselves, produces intense geological pressures leading to earthquakes, avalanches and volcanic eruptions, either onshore or beneath the sea's surface. When the tremors occur in the depths of the ocean, giant offshore oscillations sweep in as terrifying sea waves, like the coup de grace that completes the earthquake's destruction on land.

Along South America's 4000-mile Pacific coast, the great waves are called maremotos ("moving water")—first cousins to terremotos ("moving earth"). English-speakers know them as tsunami and earthquakes. For geological ages past, these closely related phenomena have afflicted the South American region stretching from the deep offshore Peru-Chile Trench to the Cordillera de los Andes—as they will continue to do for ages to come. Over the centuries, the last sensation for untold thousands of coastal residents has been the earth beneath them rolling and tossing like waves, or the horrifying vision of a surging tsunami looming from the sea to engulf them.

The Pacific coasts of Chile and Peru comprise the most unsta-

ble segment of the dangerous "ring of fire," an extended seismic zone encircling most of the Pacific Basin to include Japan and the Aleutians. Chile and Peru endure more earthquakes and volcanic eruptions per square mile than any other part of the world. In the 20th century alone, one in every three Pacific-wide tsunami originated in the Chile-Peru sector, while Chile alone accounted for 40 percent of all damaging tsunami reported in the world.

Physical Features of Tsunami

Unlike ordinary wind-generated surface waves, tsunami are true gravity waves with exceptionally long lengths and periods. The tsunami is not a single wave, but a series or "train" of giant oscillations, similar to but incomparably larger than ripples radiating out from a pebble dropped in the water. More than 150 miles can separate two successive crests, which in open sea may average only two or three feet in height. With a slope this gradual, the waves go unfelt by passing ships.

Coastal topography determines how the tsunami makes landfall. If deep water extends close inshore, the waves' impact will be minimal, but will exceed high-tide levels like a vast surging flood. However, if the sea floor slopes gradually up to the coast, the great waves begin to "feel the bottom." This bottom friction slows their forward momentum, causing a "bunching-up" as successive waves are pushed closer together. The "killer" in a tsunami train is often somewhere between the third and eighth waves, as displaced kinetic energy is transferred upward into towering walls of water, sometimes exceeding 100 feet in height. The worst possible coastal scenario is the V-shaped harbor, where the force of an incoming tsunami is concentrated and funneled into a sea wave of monstrous proportions. The hapless city of Arica, directly in the crotch of the "Big Bend," has suffered severely many times as a result—more than any other location on South America's Pacific coast.

The first sign of an incoming tsunami train is often an ominous withdrawal of the sea from the shore—a massive outflow of water far beyond the limits of dead low tide which occurs when a seismic trough, rather than a crest, reaches land. As the water recedes, a cacophony of hissing, rattling, sucking and boiling sounds can be heard as pebbles, rocks, shells and assorted debris are drawn out to sea. Whole bays empty in minutes, stranding myriad forms of marine life and exposing long-sunken wrecks to view. In the past, unknowing onlookers rushed out

The Ring of Fire

RUSSIA
Alaska
CANADA
JAPAN
Mt. Katmai
CHINA
Mt. Fuji
Mt. St. Helens
UNITED
STATES
MEXICO
Paricutín
Taal
Mayon
Hawaii
PHILIPPINES
Mauna Loa ▲   ▲ Kilauea
Mt. Pelée
GUAM
Ixtacihuati
Cotopaxi
Pacific Ocean
SOUTH
AMERICA
Tambora
SAMOA
AUSTRALIA
Aconcagua
NEW
ZEALAND

gleefully to examine these unexpected treasures. Few if any ever
survived their folly, for minutes later the sea returned in a tremendous surge of churning water too fast to outrun.

Seismically generated waves attain astounding speeds while
transiting an ocean. A tsunami's forward speed is directly pro-
portional to the varying depth of water through which it
passes—the deeper the water, the greater the speed. In water
20,000 feet deep, a tsunami shock wave will race along at 545
miles per hour. Moreover, depending on the original disturbance,
tsunami can cover thousands of miles before finally dissipating.
The world's longest tsunami waves come from Chile and can
travel more than 12,000 miles across the Pacific—nearly half the
world's circumference—to break against the shores of eastern
Siberia. Long-range tsunami have literally bounced off continental barriers and reflected back the way they came. In 1922, a
Chilean sea wave rebounded back and forth across the Pacific for
a week before finally disappearing.

Twenty-one years after the founding of Santiago de Chile by
the Spaniard Pedro de Valdivia, on October 28, 1562, the earliest

recorded tsunami stormed ashore along 900 miles of central Chilean coastline to either side of Concepcion and Talcahuano. Between 1562 and 1900, another 29 recorded tsunami struck the west coast of South America, with 20 more reported since 1900. The worst of these earthquake-tsunami calamities include:

- 1570: Concepcion sustains heavy earthquake damage, and is then engulfed by giant waves that destroy the city and its environs.
- 1586: Lima is shaken by earthquake, then struck by an 84-foot tsunami that inundates the coast for six miles inland.
- 1604: 1200 miles of Chilean and Peruvian coastline awash under the great waves. Arica is flooded.
- 1615: Tsunami flood Arica again.
- 1657: An earthquake centered near Santiago, Chile, generates great coastal waves between 36 degrees and 39 degrees South. Concepcion sustains three tsunami onslaughts that destroy what survived the tremors.
- 1687: Lima and Callao are shaken by earthquake; resulting waves destroy Callao.
- 1705: Earthquake strikes Arequipa and Arica; Arica is destroyed.
- 1724: Following an earthquake near Lima, 80-foot waves flood Callao and sink 19 ships.
- 1730: Tsunami waves sweep ashore along 600 miles of Chilean coastline, inundating Valparaiso. Three waves also damage Concepcion.
- 1746: Callao sustains two tsunami waves, one 80 feet high. Only 200 of 5000 inhabitants survive. All ships in the harbor are destroyed or driven ashore; one of these is carried a mile inland.
- 1751: Concepcion is destroyed for the fourth time as tsunami waves sweep ashore for 24 hours. The city is reestablished at a more sheltered location nearby.

A Report by Charles Darwin

On February 20, 1835, Charles Darwin was visiting Concepcion when a great seismic tremor hit that part of Chile. Writing in the *Voyage of the Beagle*, he reported:

> Shortly after the shock, a great wave was seen from a distance of three or four miles, approaching in the mid-

dle of the bay with a smooth outline; but along the shore it tore up cottages and trees as it swept onward with irrestible force. At the head of the bay it broke in a fearful line of white breakers which rushed up to a height of 23 vertical feet above the highest spring tides. Their force must have been prodigious, for at the fort a cannon with its carriage, estimated at four tons in weight, was moved 15 feet inward. A schooner was left in the midst of the ruins, 200 yards from the beach. The first wave was followed by two others, while their retreat carried away a vast wreck of floating objects.

In one part of the bay a ship was pitched high and dry on shore, was carried off, again driven on shore, and again carried off. In another part, two large vessels anchored near together were whirled about, and their cables were thrice wound round each other; though anchored at a depth of 36 feet, they were for some minutes aground.

In 1868, tsunami waves again charged ashore from Trujillo south to Concepcion. Iquique took a 40-foot wave that covered the city. At Talcahuano, far to the south, waves 30 feet above high tide came ashore with disastrous results. The U.S.S. *Wateree* was anchored in the roads off Arica when the earthquake struck. Ship's officers felt the deck shudder suddenly beneath them, and rushing on deck, saw the land rippling and the hills about to "capsize." Lieutenant L.G. Billings reported,

As the dust thinned out, we rubbed our eyes and stared, unable to believe what we saw: where a few seconds before, there had stood a happy and prosperous city, busy, active and full of life, we saw nothing but ruins. The ... unhappy people, caught under the wreckage of what had been their houses, were struggling among the ruins, and everywhere shrieks, cries of pain, and calls for help tore the air.

Knowing that a tsunami would soon hit, the *Wateree*'s captain hurriedly ordered a boat cast off to rescue at least some of the survivors crowding the docks. Lieutenant Billings continues:

We on board were organizing a body of men to be sent ashore ... when all at once a hoarse murmuring

noise made us look up. Looking to the land we saw, to
our horror, that where a moment before there had
been the jetty, all black with human beings, there was
nothing. Everything had been swallowed in a moment
by the sudden rising, of the sea, which the ship, floating upon it, had not noticed.

The *Wateree* survived two quakes in succession. The first produced only a moderate tsunami, but following the second, the
waters receded and stranded the *Wateree* and other ships on the
exposed sea floor. Being flat-bottomed, the *Wateree* settled upright while the other round-bottomed ships rolled over on their
sides and were swamped when the next wave surged in. Again
the ship rose and fell. As night approached, yet another tsunami
came in, this time the 70-foot breaking wave which lifted the *Wateree* on its unforgettable last "voyage" over Arica itself and into
the hinterland. When it was over, the crew could not believe that
not one of their number was lost—unlike the fate of the hapless
residents ashore. Twenty thousand inhabitants in a dozen destroyed coastal towns died.

The Far-Reaching Effects of Tsunami

In [the twentieth] century, many tsunami trains stormed South
America's Pacific coast, but few of these had the destructive impact of former years.

Nevertheless, their effects were felt severely thousands of
miles away in distant parts of the Pacific Basin. The quake that
struck in May, 1960 is a case in point—one forever seared in the
memory of all Chileans who lived through it. Six major shocks,
each with a separate epicenter, rocked the nation and took more
than 5000 lives, destroying 20 percent of Chile's industrial potential, awakening six dormant volcanoes, and giving birth to
three new volcanoes.

Loose soils, saturated by the earlier wet Southern Hemisphere
summer and autumn, undermined building stability and contributed to the widespread devastation. One observer related how
the older buildings simply "dissolved with a weary slowness like
lumps of sugar in hot tea." However, although Chile sustained
enormous earthquake damage, the tsunamis generated by the
tremors wreaked greatest havoc elsewhere. The waves reached
the farthest corners of the Pacific, and despite Tsunami Warning
System alerts, took the lives of many in Hawaii and Japan who

thought they were safe from harm by virtue of their distance from the source.

Tsunami share the category of "rapid-onset natural hazards" along with earthquakes, landslides, hurricanes, tornadoes, floods, volcanic eruptions, and wildfires. In the last 20 years, these natural catastrophes have claimed 2.8 million lives and affected 820 million others. In [the twentieth] century, 94 recorded tsunami events killed more than 51,000 coastal residents; 90 percent of these fatalities occurred within 250 miles of the originating earthquake's epicenter. As with other natural disasters, man is incapable of preventing the occurrence of tsunami, so efforts to mitigate their disastrous impact have focused on early warning systems to enable prompt evacuation of areas most likely to be affected.

Tsunami Warning Systems

The first efforts in this regard took place in response to a surprise seismic wave which hit the Aleutian and Hawaiian Islands on April 1, 1946 and took more than 160 lives. The U.S. government created a tsunami early-warning system to alert the entire Pacific basin of future tsunami threats. In 1948, the Seismic Sea Wave Warning System went into effect, which subsequently evolved into the Tsunami Warning System (TWS).

The first TWS took one hour to receive and evaluate tsunami reports and issue warnings. This was an adequate response time for threatened populations more than 465 miles from approaching wave trains, but there were regions (such as Hawaii, Alaska and Japan) where faster warnings were needed. A modified plan was then developed, called the Regional Tsunami Warning System, that generated alerts within ten minutes of verification— more than enough time for populations located 60 to 465 miles from a local tsunami.

But one region still remained unserved by even the Regional TWS. Chile, the most chronically seismic area of all, required notice of tsunamis emanating less than 62 miles away from population centers. By the mid-1980's, a sophisticated warning system tailored to meet the Chilean challenge went into service. Project THRUST (for Tsunami Hazards Reduction Utilizing Systems Technology) employs satellite communications to provide an incredible two-minute tsunami response time.

Project THRUST has not yet had to respond to a major tsunami threat, but it's only a matter of time before it does.

William Berninghausen, of the Marine Science Department of the U.S. Naval Oceanographic Office, observes that tsunami occur with regularity along South America's Pacific coast, sometimes as frequently as once every three years. Even with the early warning systems in place, the potential for tremendous losses from the waves increases every year as coastal population centers continue to grow and diversify. We can only prepare ourselves for the worst, and acknowledge nature's ultimate power to impose her own will. As David Ritchie, author of *The Ring of Fire*, observes:

> Once the wave ripples out from the site of a quake or eruption, all we can do is to try to get out of the way. We can send astronauts to the moon, land robots on Mars and Venus, defeat epidemic disease, and crack the very chemistry of life itself, but with all our science and technology, we cannot stop a single ripple in the basin.

Tsunami Disasters

The Grounding of the USS *Wateree*

By Ernest Zebrowski Jr.

In August of 1868, the crewmen of the USS Wateree *sat helpessly anchored on the west coast of South America as a monstrous tsunami swiftly advanced toward them. Other boats anchored nearby with less sturdy construction had crashed into cliffs along the harbor with the first surge of incoming waves. As Ernest Zebrowski Jr. recounts, this gigantic wave, later measured at seventy feet high, carried the flat-bottomed boat almost two miles inland, where the* Wateree *eventually rested, unharmed but mired permanently in the sand. The tsunami continued to travel at an estimated speed of five hundred miles per hour for more than twelve and a half hours and crashed onto the shores of the Sandwich Islands (Hawaii) more than five thousand nautical miles away. Scientists believe the tsunami was generated by the aftershocks of an undersea earthquake close to shore. The earthquake leveled the port town of Arica and, along with the tsunami, was responsible for twenty-five thousand deaths.*

Ernest Zebrowski Jr. is a professor of science and mathematics-education. Zebrowski lectures and writes extensively about natural disasters and has authored several books including Perils of a Restless Planet.

A crew of 235 Americans on the man-of-war *U.S.S. Wateree* had a firsthand experience with a tsunami that many of us would be inclined to dismiss as a fabrication if the documentation weren't so compelling. This ship surfed on the crest of a tsunami and came to rest in the Atacama Desert some 4 kilometers (3 mi) up the coast and 3 kilometers (nearly 2 mi) inland from its initial anchorage. . . . The *Wateree* came to rest upright and intact, with the loss of only one crewman, who had been in a small lifeboat at the time. Inhabitants of the coastal cities

Ernest Zebrowski Jr., *Perils of a Restless Planet: Scientific Perspectives on Natural Disasters*. Cambridge, UK: Cambridge University Press, 1997. Copyright © 1997 by Cambridge University Press. Reproduced by permission.

of Arica and Iquique didn't fare nearly as well; some 25,000 lost their lives to this tsunami and the earthquake that preceded it.

The *Wateree* was one of a class of ships built in the United States at the close of the Civil War to navigate the shallow rivers of the South; for this reason it was flat-bottomed and double-ended, like a canoe. The Civil War ended before the boat could be used for its intended purpose, and it was sent on a cruise to the southern Pacific and the western coast of South America. In August of 1868 the ship was anchored in the harbor at Arica, in what is now northern Chile, while its boilers and engines were being overhauled in preparation for a return cruise to San Francisco. Arica, with a population of some 10,000 at that time, was the terminus of the only railroad connecting the coast with Bolivia and therefore had become a center for the machine shops necessary to serve both rolling stock and ships.

When the Earthquake Struck

The earthquake struck at around 4 P.M. on August 13, and the initial tremors were felt aboard the ship. Most of the crew ran on deck and watched in horror as the town swayed like the "waves of a troubled sea," then collapsed in a great cloud of dust. The waters of the harbor began to surge and slosh, dragging the international collection of anchored boats in unpredictable directions and smashing some into the cliffs that bordered the harbor. Survivors from the city crowded onto the pier and were quickly swept away by a huge swell in the harbor. The Peruvian man-of-war *America* hastily got up a head of steam and attempted to get out to sea, but to no avail. In the words of Rear Admiral L.G. Billings, recounting the event many years later,

> this time the sea receded until the shipping was left stranded, while as far to seaward as our vision could reach, we saw the rocky bottom of the sea, never before exposed to human gaze, with struggling fish and monsters of the deep left high and dry. The round-bottomed ships keeled over on their beam ends, while the *Wateree* rested easily on her floor-like bottom; and when the returning sea, not like a wave, but rather like an enormous tide, came sweeping back, rolling our unfortunate companion ships over and over, leaving some bottom up and others masses of wreckage, the *Wateree* rose easily over the tossing waters, unharmed.

Billings's account also describes how this returning wave swallowed up a fort and completely washed away its Peruvian garrison and a number of 15-inch cannons weighing several tons apiece. All of this fits the description of a tsunami generated by an undersea earthquake centered fairly close to shore. The *Wateree*'s captain, however, must have been a very cautious man, for he prepared the crew for more to come. Returning to Billings's words,

> It had now been dark for some time and we knew not where we were, the absence of the usual beacon and shore lights adding to our confusion. About 8:30 P.M. the lookout hailed the deck and reported a breaker approaching. Looking seaward, we saw, first, a thin line of phosphorescent light, which loomed higher and higher until it seemed to touch the sky; its crest, crowned with the death light of phosphorescent glow, showing the sullen masses of water below. Heralded by the thundering roar of a thousand breakers combined, the dreaded tidal wave was upon us at last. Of all the horrors of this dreadful time, this seemed the worst. Chained to the spot, helpless to escape, with all the preparations made which human skill could suggest, we could but watch the monster wave approach without the sustaining help of action. We could only grip the life-line and await the coming catastrophe.

The Height of the Waves

The ship came to rest in the sand 3 kilometers inland and just 60 meters short of being dashed against a cliff. The next morning, the ship's navigator measured the high water mark on the adjacent mountain at 14.3 meters (47 ft) above the sand, "not including the comb" of the wave (although it is not clear how the latter was established). The U.S. Coast and Geodetic Survey has since estimated the tsunami's height at approximately 21 meters (70 ft) at the time it struck the *Wateree*. In Arica, this wave swept away heavy pieces of machine shop equipment and even complete railroad trains, including their locomotives, leaving behind no trace.

At Iquique, 193 kilometers (120 mi) to the south, the receding wave uncovered the bay to a depth of 7.3 meters (24 ft) and returned with a 12-meter (40-ft) wave crest that engulfed the city.

The earthquake that generated the wave permanently raised sections of the shoreline between Arica and Iquique as much as 6 meters (20 ft). The tsunami was recorded at the Sandwich Islands, 5,580 nautical miles distant, only 12 hours and 37 minutes after it struck Arica. In order for the wave to travel this far this fast, the average wave speed had to have been some 800 kilometers per hour (500 mi/h)! Modern jetliners don't travel much faster.

A Series of Two Tsunamis

Every attempt to base a scientific interpretation on eyewitness accounts is, admittedly, problematic. If we take Billings's account at face value, however, it would appear that he and his fellow crewmen experienced not one series of tsunamis, but two. There was too much of a time lag, more than 4 hours, between the earthquake and the last great wave for the two events to have had a simple connection. A more reasonable scenario is this: One of the earthquake's aftershocks (Billings's account mentions a number of these) may have triggered an underwater landslide off the continental shelf, perhaps offshore of the mouth of the Uuta River, where silt could easily have been accumulating for centuries. It would have required only a relatively mild aftershock to produce a devastating tsunami in this manner, particularly if the accumulation of silt had already been rendered unstable by the prior earthquake. The possibility of such a delayed effect suggests that it may not be prudent for a population to consider the seas safe from tsunamis until many hours, or even days, after an earthquake.

And what happened to the *Wateree* and her crew? The stranded sailors were rescued three weeks later by the U.S. frigate *Powhatan*, which was making a scheduled stop. The *Wateree*, though undamaged, was hopelessly mired in the sand much too far from the sea for there to be any hope of refloating the ship. It was sold at auction to a hotel company, then used successively as a hospital and warehouse, finally succumbing to destruction by artillery during the Peruvian-Chilean War. The remains of its iron ribs have since disappeared into the shifting desert sands of what is today northern Chile.

The Most Deadly Tsunami: Krakatau of 1883

By Edward Bryant

The eruption of Krakatau's volcano in 1883 created the most deadly tsunamis in recorded history, killing an estimated thirty-six thousand people. In this piece, physical geographer Edward Bryant recounts the unique experience of a Dutch volcanologist named Van Guest who climbed through the jungles above the town of Anjer Lor in the Indonesian Islands and watched as the volcano and tsunamis devastated the town. With a handkerchief tied over his nose and mouth to protect him from the sulfurous fumes, the volcanologist peered through his telescope and witnessed the destructive waves flooding the land. As he observed the tsunamis, a blast of air flattened the scientist, and the largest explosion ever heard generated shock waves that circled the globe seven times.

V an Guest was sweating profusely as he climbed through the dense jungle above the town of Anjer Lor. He stopped to gasp for breath, not because he was slightly out of shape, but because the sulphurous fumes burned his lungs. He looked down at the partially ruined town. There was no sign of life although it was nearly 10 o'clock. His head pounded as the excitement of the scene and the strain of the trek sped blood through his temples. He did not know if he felt the thumping of blood in his head or the distant rumbling. Sometimes both were synchronous, and it made him smile. This was the chance of a lifetime. No one was paid to do what he did or had remotely thought to climb to the top of one of the hills to get the best view. Besides, most of the townspeople had fled into the jungle after the waves had come through yesterday and again in the early morning. As he neared the top of the hill he looked for a spot with a clearing to the west, reached it, and turned. Beyond lay purgatory on Earth, the incredible hell of Krakatau in full eruption.

The Town Cleared Out by Tsunamis

As a volcanologist for the Dutch colonial government, Van Guest was aware of the many eruptions that continually threatened Dutch interests in the East Indies. Tambora in 1815 was the worst. No one thought that anything else could be bigger. He had seen Galunggung go up the previous year with over a hundred villages wiped out. Krakatau had had an earthquake then, and when it began to erupt in May [1883], the governor in Batavia had ordered him to investigate. He had come to this side of the Sunda Strait because he thought he would be safe 40 km from the eruption. Van Guest tied his handkerchief over his nose and mouth, slipped on the goggles to keep the sting from his eyes, and peered through his telescope across the strait, hoping to catch a glimpse of the volcano itself through the ash and smoke. Suddenly the view cleared as if a strong wind had blown the sky clean. He could see the ocean frothing and churning chaotically. Only the Rakata peak remained, and it was glowing red. The smallest peak, Perboewatan, had blown up at 5:30 that morning. Danan, which was 450 m high, had gone just over an hour later. Each had sent out a tsunami striking the coastline of Java and Sumatra in the dark. That is what had cleared out the town in the early hours.

Experiencing the Explosion and Monstrous Wave

As he glanced down at the abandoned boats in the bay, Van Guest noticed that they were all lining up towards the volcano. Then they drifted quickly out to sea and disappeared in the maelstrom. Suddenly, a bolt of yellow opened in the ocean running across the strait to the northwest and all the waters in the strait flooded in. Instantly, a cloud of steam rose to the top of the sky. As Van Guest stood upright, awestruck, a blast of air flattened him to the ground and an incredible noise deafened him. The largest explosion ever heard by humans had just swept over him. The shock wave would circle the globe seven times. When he gained his feet, Van Guest thought he was blind. The whole sky was as black as night. He stumbled down the slope back towards the town. It took him nearly 30 minutes to get down to the edge of the town through the murk. Just as he approached the outskirts of Anjer Lor, he could see the telegraph master, panic-stricken, racing up the hill towards him, silhouetted against the sea—or what Van Guest thought was the sea. It was hilly and moving fast towards him. The sea slowly reared up into an incredible wave over 15 m high and smashed through the remains of buildings next to the shoreline. Within seconds it had splintered through the rest of the houses in the town and was closing fast. The pace of the telegraph master slowed noticeably as he climbed the hill. The wave crashed through the coconut palms and jungle at the edge of the town. Tossing debris into the air, it sloshed up the hill. The telegraph master kept running or stumbling towards Van Guest, then collapsed into his arms with only metres to spare between him and the wave. It had finally stopped. Both men had just witnessed one of the biggest volcanic eruptions and tsunami ever recorded.

The Twentieth Century's Largest Tsunami

The largest tsunami of the twentieth century hit Hawaii on April Fools' Day in 1946. The monster wave killed 159 people in the Hawaiian area, including twenty-five schoolchildren. The author, associate geophysicist Gerard Fryer, believes that the deaths could have been avoided if people had understood what a tsunami was and had fled to safety. Seismologists and oceanographers traced the source of the tsunami to an earthquake close to Unimak Island in the Aleutian Islands, southwest of Alaska. The tsunamis generated from the earthquake spread concentrically, shaking the entire Pacific Ocean and continuing to cause unusual tide levels three days later.

Marsue McGinnis woke just before seven o'clock to the sound of shouting. Outside the cottage, children were calling out, "Come see the tidal wave!" It must be a prank, she decided; probably some of her early–rising pupils on their way to school. April fool. McGinnis and her housemates, Dorothy Drake, Fay Johnson and Helen Kingseed, also roused by the shouts, hurried out onto the porch.

It was April 1, 1946. The four novice teachers had come to Hawai'i in the postwar euphoria of the previous year and had been assigned to a school on Laupahoehoe Point, a low lava peninsula jutting into the Pacific from the wooded cliffs of the Big Island's Hamakua coast. Their cottage, one of five strung along the shoreline, lay just a short walk across a green park from the main school buildings, which nestled at the foot of the cliff 200 yards away.

The children had been telling the truth: the ocean was receding. The sea level fell past the normal low-water mark and kept falling until a swath of rocky seafloor lay exposed. Then the water returned, hissing with turbulence, flooding the road in front of the cottages. Again the sea receded, and again it rose, flooding the land. Everyone watched in fascination. Could this be a rare twin tidal wave? As the water sucked out even farther than before, a carnival atmosphere took hold; children and teachers happily explored the dry seafloor, picking up stranded fish.

Tiring of the novelty, Drake and Kingseed returned to their delayed preparations for the school day. On the porch McGinnis and Johnson agreed it was a shame that, unlike Dorothy Lamour in the South Seas movies, they had not experienced a really big wave. They soon would. Taking a snapshot of the children near the shore, McGinnis saw through the viewfinder a wave racing toward shore, forming a wall of water that grew as it approached. Alarmed, she and Johnson dashed into the house to warn the others.

The Wave Hits Shore

They were too late. In seconds, the women were awash in roaring turbulent water boiling with sand. The cottage was shattered; all that remained intact was the roof, which floated fifteen feet above what had been dry land. The wave churned across the park, smashed through the school washroom and spent itself at the foot of the main school building. Then the water started draining away, dragging with it cars, trees, pigs, chickens, broken buildings and people. The cottage roof was swept seaward, McGinnis and Johnson clinging to its top and Drake clutching one corner.

Kingseed had died in the first rush of water. Drake, exhausted and panic stricken, lost her grip on the roof and was swept away. Then the water fell, and the roof crashed to a stop on jutting rocks. Johnson and McGinnis slipped off and started to wade toward shore. Just when they were almost to safety, the next wave swept them up and beat them down on the jagged lava spires near the point. Johnson disappeared. McGinnis, a strong swimmer, struggled to the surface to snatch a breath before the backwash tumbled her through the rocks and dragged her out to sea. It was eight o'clock.

Nine hours later, McGinnis was picked up, bruised, dazed,

bleeding and seasick, by one of the few local boats that the waves had left seaworthy enough to risk a rescue mission. She was exceptionally lucky. In all, only four survivors were picked up from the water; three more were helped to shore the following day, miles from cliffbound Laupahoehoe. Throughout the Hawaiian Islands the watery onslaught had claimed 159 lives. In Hilo, twenty-five miles southeast of Laupahoehoe, the waves had caused ninety-six deaths as they wrecked the city's waterfront. In Laupahoehoe twenty-five people had died; most of them were children, Marsue McGinnis's pupils.

The Real Killer Is Ignorance

What hit Hawai'i in April 1946 was a tsunami, the largest of this century. Since then the scientific understanding of tsunamis has increased dramatically. Thanks to a huge increase in seismic data, to new seafloor-mapping techniques and to increasingly sophisticated computer models, seismologists and oceanographers now understand in detail where tsunamis come from, how they propagate across the open ocean and what forces shape them when they reach shore. Public awareness of tsunamis, however, has lagged far behind. The real killer at Laupahoehoe was not water but ignorance: with a little more knowledge, the victims could have recognized the ocean's warning signs and reached safety. Unfortunately, since then the tragedy has replayed itself many times over. In 1960 and 1964 in Alaska, California and Hawai'i, for instance, hundreds of lives were needlessly lost to tsunamis despite abundant warning, and there is every reason to think that the same thing could happen tomorrow. The best early-warning system in the world cannot protect someone who does not understand what a tsunami is.

The common term tidal wave is a dangerous misnomer. A tsunami has nothing to do with tides; nor is it a single wave, as the people of Laupahoehoe learned at great cost. A tsunami can be triggered by a submarine volcanic eruption, a landslide or, most commonly, an earthquake—anything that suddenly causes a large disruption in the sea level (including, very rarely, a meteorite impact). Uplift the seafloor by, say, ten feet, and you create a ten-foot-high mound of excess water at the surface. Such a mound will collapse under gravity to generate the tsunami—a succession of waves that radiate outward across the surface of the ocean like ripples in a pond.

Understanding Wave Mechanics

Making ripples in a pond is an excellent way of teaching your-self elementary wave mechanics. As a teenager in Malaysia, I used to drop rocks off a cliff into a muddy lake that appeared at a building site after heavy rain. Small pebbles, I noticed, sent little ripples expanding sedately across the lake. The waves from a boulder, in contrast, traveled more than twice as fast and had wavelengths (the distances from one crest to the next) perhaps ten times as long. As the lake dried up, the waves from big rocks got slower and changed in character. In a foot of water, individual wave crests advanced to the leading edge of the expanding disturbance and disappeared. But when the depth of the water dropped to an inch or so, the waves would travel across the full thirty-foot length of the lake and wash up on the shorelines, staining the water red with laterite mud. Then they would reflect back across the lake and reflect again, creating a jumble of criss-crossing patterns.

Years later I learned that what makes shallow-water waves so special has to do with the way minute parcels of water move when a wave passes. Ordinary waves set water moving in vertical loops, which get tighter with depth and dwindle away entirely at depths greater than half a wavelength. In shallow water, however, the oscillations reach all the way to the bottom. In a sense, the waves can "feel" the bottom, and as a result they move through the water differently from their deepwater cousins.

Shallow-Water Waves

Bizarre as it might sound, tsunamis are shallow-water waves. They have wavelengths so inconceivably long—seventy to 300 miles from crest to crest—that even in the three-mile depths of the open ocean, the waves set the entire water column in motion, just like a boulder heaved into an inch-deep pond. One result is that tsunamis move surface water farther than ordinary waves do, sometimes enough to set it rocking back and forth as much as thirty feet. Another is that the interaction with the bottom limits their speed. In a bottomless ocean the speed of a wave would depend only on its wavelength, and tsunamis would sweep across the surface at more than a thousand miles an hour. Once waves start to feel the bottom, however, their speed is controlled by the depth of the water. As a result a tsunami crosses a three-mile-deep ocean at just under 500 miles an hour, slightly slower than the cruising speed of a Boeing 747.

Yet despite their enormous speed and energy, tsunamis are imperceptible on the open ocean. They typically have a period (the time from one wave crest to the next) of between nine and thirty minutes and an amplitude of a foot or two at most. The waves of 1946 had a fifteen-minute period and were no more than two feet high in the deep ocean, much too slow and gentle a motion to be sensed from a ship. Indeed, the captain of a merchant ship off Hilo in 1946 reported that he could not feel the waves that he saw crashing on shore.

Only when a tsunami reaches shore does it reveal itself as the alien being it really is. The classic artist's conception—a surfer's dream wave scaled up to a hundred feet high—is dead wrong. True, tsunami waves grow as they approach a shoreline, for much the same reason as normal waves do: interaction with a shoaling bottom slows the wave, shortening its wavelength; to transport the same amount of energy, the wave must get taller. But there the resemblance to ordinary surf ends.

Even very large normal waves, such as the twenty-foot monsters that draw surfers to O'ahu's northern shore, exhaust their energy close to the shoreline. A two-foot-high, hundred-mile-long, 500-mile-an-hour tsunami wave rushing toward shore, however, creates a vastly different effect. As its wavelength crumples to about five miles, the wave grows to ten feet in height. The front of the wave, in shallow offshore water, suddenly slows to about twenty miles an hour, while the back of the wave, still in thousand-foot-deep water, keeps barreling along at almost full speed. The wave rushes up onto the beach without breaking and can ravage low-lying areas half a mile inland. In the largest tsunamis, the crest of a wave may roll forward to form a turbulent wall of water with higher water behind—a bore. Bores are particularly common late in the tsunami sequence, when return flow from one wave collides with the next incoming wave. A bore is what destroyed McGinnis's cottage at Laupahoehoe.

What Triggered the Tsunami of 1946?

What triggered the tsunami of April 1, 1946? Seismologists and oceanographers have traced its source back thousands of miles from Hawai'i, to the eastern Aleutian Islands. The first human settlement to have a taste of what was to come was a Coast Guard station on Scotch Cap, a rocky headland at the south-western extremity of Unimak Island. At 1:29 A.M. (1:59 A.M. Hawai'i time, according to the system then in effect) the five guardsmen inside the Scotch Cap lighthouse felt a sudden, severe earthquake lasting almost a minute. Forty-seven minutes later the first of a series of monstrous waves engulfed the lighthouse and crested the cliff behind the building, flooding the station's sleeping quarters and forcing the men there to flee. At dawn the men returned to find a scene of incomprehensible destruction. The lighthouse had been sheared off at its base, broken into pieces and scattered over the bluff to an elevation of 115 feet. Of its five-man crew there was no trace.

The waves that had raked Unimak spread concentrically across the Pacific. As one front battered Laupahoehoe and Hilo, another rolled down the California coast, flooding buildings, damaging boats and piers, and sweeping to his death a man on the beach at Santa Cruz. Hours later, Japan reported a run-up (the maximum height a tsunami wave reaches as it rushes ashore) of three feet. Samoa reported seven feet; the Marquesas Islands [islands in French Polynesia], thirty feet; Talara in Peru, eighteen inches. At Iquique, Chile, seventeen hours after the earthquake and nearly 9,000 miles from the epicenter, waves swamped fishing boats at their moorings. Almost everywhere, the tsunami seemed to die down after several hours, only to reappear with the arrival of waves reflected off some distant shore. The reflections were followed by re-reflections; three days after the earthquake, tide gauges in Hawai'i, Samoa and New Zealand still registered unusual variations in the sea level. The entire Pacific, more than a third of the earth's surface area, was quivering.

The 1998 Papua New Guinea Tsunami

By Walter C. Dudley and Min Lee

The 1998 Papua New Guinea tsunami will long be remembered as one of the worst tragedies to strike that area in its history. Minutes after an earthquake struck near New Guinea, a Pacific island north of Australia, the Pacific Tsunami Warning Center issued a bulletin announcing there was no destructive Pacific-wide tsunami threat. Soon afterward, three undetected, local tsunamis crashed along a twenty mile stretch of shoreline, inundating local villages. The tsunamis claimed the lives of an estimated two thousand people, injured hundreds of others, and left five thousand people homeless. In the grim aftermath, efforts at recovering bodies at sea, some of which had been carried as far as one hundred miles, were complicated by the pollution of ocean water and the threat of disease. Aid came to the area from around the world in the form of food, equipment, and medical supplies. Ironically, a lumber company donated lumber to rebuild village schools, but schools may not be necessary for years to come because nearly an entire generation of children has been killed.

Walter C. Dudley is a professor of oceanography at the University of Hawaii and a media contact for the International Tsunami Information Center in Honolulu. Min Lee is a writer who interviewed tsunami survivors in Hawaii and collected their stories from 1978 to 1985 and again in 1996.

T he year 1997 and the first half of 1998 were relatively quiet [in terms of tsunamis], but then on July 17, 1998, a tsunami disaster struck the island of New Guinea, this

Walter C. Dudley and Min Lee, *Tsunami!* Honolulu: University of Hawaii Press, 1998. Copyright © 1998 by University of Hawaii Press. Reproduced by permission.

time affecting the country of Papua New Guinea on the eastern half of the island. Papua New Guinea is a nation of some 4 million people, where many of the tribes still live a subsistence-based agricultural lifestyle. The El Niño of 1997/1998 had produced a serious drought in the region. Crops suffered, famine threatened, and the drying up of streams that are often the only source of water for drinking, cooking, and washing, resulted in serious health problems. Just as the country was beginning to recover from the El Niño, a disastrous tsunami crashed ashore along its northern coast.

At 6:49 P.M. local time, an earthquake registering 7.1 on the Richter Scale rocked the ocean floor at the western end of the Bismark Sea, just offshore of the village of Aitape in West Sepik province, one of the most remote and isolated parts of New Guinea, and some 370 miles northwest of Port Moresby. Villagers reported their homes shaking from the tremors, but because most structures were made of materials gathered from the jungle, especially palm fronds, there was little in the way of damage. Nonetheless, the villagers were left with a sense of foreboding. Although this is a seismically active region of the Pacific, the local area had experienced only relatively moderate earthquakes in recent history, with but nine major earthquakes (magnitude greater than 7.5) occurring since 1900. A magnitude 7 earthquake had struck the area in December 1907, causing a stretch of coastline about 25 kilometers west of Aitape to subside, creating a large, shallow lagoon between 6 and 13 feet deep, which was named Sissano Lagoon. The same area was again struck in 1935 by a 7.9 earthquake, which may have generated a small tsunami. Though there appears to be no native lore of either of these events, the 1998 tsunami will long be remembered as one of the greatest tragedies ever to strike the region.

Within minutes after the earthquake, the Pacific Tsunami Warning Center had issued the following bulletin:

THIS IS A TSUNAMI INFORMATION MESSAGE, NO ACTION REQUIRED. AN EARTHQUAKE, PRELIMINARY MAGNITUDE 7.1, OCCURRED AT 0850 17 JULY 1998, LOCATED NEAR LATITUDE 2S LONGITUDE 142E IN THE VICINITY OF NORTH OF NEW GUINEA.

EVALUATION: NO DESTRUCTIVE PACIFIC-WIDE TSUNAMI THREAT EXISTS.

The Tsunami Waves Hit

Yet with its shallow focus at a depth of between only 10 and 20 miles, the earthquake proved very efficient at generating a deadly local tsunami. Beginning shortly after 7 P.M. the first of three tsunami waves began to crash ashore, inundating a 20-mile stretch of beach extending from west of Aitape to the village of Serai. The worst damage was at the four villages of Sissano, Warapu, Arop, and Malol. All four villages were built on beaches, and their wooden huts were only a few feet above sea level. Warapu and Arop were especially vulnerable, situated between the Pacific Ocean and Sissano Lagoon on a narrow spit of land only 100 yards wide.

Many villagers spoke of hearing sounds like those made by jet fighters, just before the turbulent water surged through their villages. Some residents were crushed in their huts, others buried under sand and debris, while most may have drowned. At Warapu and Arop nothing was left standing, both villages completely washed away into either Sissano Lagoon or the Pacific Ocean.

Unfortunate Timing

The timing of the event added to the tragedy. Most of the village children were at home on a school holiday with their families, not staying as they normally did at the mission schools farther inland. The children were torn from their parents' arms as they all tried to flee the area. As in other tsunamis, the very young and very old numbered high among the casualties. They were too slow to run from the waves and too weak to climb coconut trees before being overwhelmed by the tsunami. The highest waves have been estimated at between 25 and 33 feet, enough to completely inundate the coastal villages.

Early reports told of 70 deaths, but this estimate was quickly and frequently revised upward. Government sources placed the official death toll at 1,600; but with 2,000 still missing, this number was expected to rise, and many people felt that the final death toll would never be accurately known. Initially there had been hope that some of the missing would be found, as many villagers had reportedly fled inland and were thought to be huddled in small groups deep in the jungle. But as time passed and more bodies were discovered, hopes began to fade.

Of the survivors, many suffered from severe injuries sustained when they were thrown against trees and debris or impaled on

A 1998 earthquake triggered tsunamis that devastated Papua New Guinea. An estimated two thousand people were killed and five thousand were left homeless.

sharp mangrove limbs and projecting roots. Others suffered from pneumonia, having inhaled water and then spent hours floating in the sea. Local medical facilities were quickly overwhelmed. Government officials reported that more than 550 people were critically injured. The 120-bed hospital at Vanimo treated more than 600 patients, with many lying on makeshift beds on the grass outside the hospital while awaiting treatment. Australia and New Zealand dispatched teams of doctors and nurses, and a portable field hospital was airlifted into the area. Local airstrips had been flooded by the tsunami, so aid was flown into the airstrip at Vanimo about 60 miles away, near the Indonesia border. As medical personnel began to treat the injuries, they found many broken bones as well as head and chest injuries; almost all the injured had lacerations. Bacteria-laden coral sand had infected the wounds, and gangrene had begun to set in. By the middle of the week following the disaster, doctors had been forced to amputate limbs from 22 men, women, and children. One doctor described the injuries as resembling battlefield wounds, and medical personnel began to worry that many of the tsunami survivors might die from infection or tropical diseases. The search for the living continued as four highly-trained "sniffer" dogs and their handlers from the Florida Rescue and Response Center were flown in to search the areas surrounding Sissano, Warapu, Arop, and Malol.

Help from Around the World

News of the disaster spread around the world, and expressions of sympathy began to pour in. Pope John Paul II dedicated his Sunday prayers to the victims, and Queen Elizabeth II, who is head of the Commonwealth and consequently also queen of Papua New Guinea, sent a message of condolence and sympathy to the people of the Aitape area. Even Papua New Guinea rebel leader Joseph Kabui requested that the people be told of his "deep sympathy." Nearly 5,000 people had been left homeless by the disaster, and aid for the survivors began to roll in. Steamship companies pledged to deliver relief supplies free of charge. Rotary International sent container-loads of medical supplies and equipment, and tarpaulins, ropes, water containers, and blankets. Chevron Oil Company loaned two aircraft and two nurses to the relief efforts, and the Australian Surfers Sunrise Club donated 24 rough-terrain wheelchairs for the amputees. Yet, confusion and lack of coordination threatened to disrupt relief efforts. Much of the food and supplies began piling up in warehouses in Aitape and Vanimo instead of being distributed. Part of the problem may have been that regional public servants, churches, and private aid organizations did not approve of the command structure set up under the state of emergency. There had simply not been adequate planning for a disaster of such magnitude.

The Search for Bodies

As time passed, emergency rescue and evacuation efforts were replaced by searching for bodies and burying the dead. An estimated 500 bodies had been seen floating in Sissano Lagoon and the sea offshore, not counting the ones scattered through the mangrove swamps. Scavengers were drawn to the area to feed on the corpses, sharks and saltwater crocodiles in the water, pigs and wild dogs along the shore. Some 200 bodies were discovered more than 100 miles to the west in Jayapura, Indonesia, where residents avoided swimming in coastal waters or buying fish in the local markets.

As the search for bodies continued, it became impossible to identify the grossly disfigured victims, so authorities merely tried to keep count. Fear of disease began to take precedence over recovering the bodies, so rescue workers quickly either cremated the corpses with gasoline or buried them in shallow graves dug where the bodies were found. The Melanesian Council of Churches observed a special day of prayer for the victims, but this was a poor substitute for traditional burial ceremonies where family members spend time weeping over the bodies and telling stories. Papua New Guinea Defense Forces were planning to string barbed wire around the devastated areas in order to keep grieving survivors from returning to their villages to bury relatives and pick through the wreckage. As ponds, wells, and other freshwater sources became polluted, the risk of disease increased; government authorities made plans to evacuate survivors, relief workers, police, and military forces and then to seal off the area. Sissano Lagoon would be declared a mass graveyard. Colonel Kanene of the Papua New Guinea Defense Forces speculated that after the bodies had decomposed for a month or so, the narrow sandbar separating the lagoon from the sea might be blown up to allow the ocean to flush the remains out to sea and disinfect the area.

Researchers Survey the Site

As with other recent tsunamis, plans were made to bring in a survey team of experts to see what might be learned from the disaster. Under the direction of Dr. Fumihiko Imamura of the Disaster Control Research Center at Tohoku University in Sendai, Japan, the team was to include seismologists, civil engineers, and tsunami experts from Japan, Australia, New Zealand, Russia, and the U. S. who would travel to the scene of the disaster after rescue operations had terminated. The scientists planned to study evidence such as sand deposits, stripped vegetation, debris on trees or wires, and water marks, as well as to record eyewitness accounts. They would produce maps showing the areas of inundation and try to determine what factors could have influenced this tsunami.

Almost from the beginning, some aspects of the tsunami resembled the local tsunamis in Nicaragua in 1992 and East Java in 1994. In each of these cases, a moderate-sized earthquake had generated a deadly local tsunami. What had caused such destructive wave run-up? Had a submarine landslide contributed to the tsunami? Or as Dr. Viacheslav Gusiaskov, head of the Tsunami Laboratory in Novosibirsk, Russia, speculated, one possible factor might have been "the presence of large depths (as much as 2½ miles deep) located close to the coastline." The survey would be important in answering many of these questions. But as the threat of disease grew, an on-site survey seemed less and less likely, and the scientists began to consider surveying the site by helicopters and taking photos and videos of the inundated areas.

As happens so often, there was an ironic twist to events in the aftermath of the tsunami. One of the donations to the stricken area was from the Stettin Bay Lumber Company, which gave lumber to rebuild local village schools destroyed during the tsunami. The tragedy is that there may be no need for new schools for many years to come, and even the mission schools that survived the tsunami may be closed. There are almost no children left to attend school. Nearly an entire generation was wiped out by the tsunami.

Chapter 3

Averting Disaster

Reducing the Risks of Tsunamis to the Coastal United States

BY ERIC L. GEIST, GUY R. GELFENBAUM,
BRUCE E. JAFFE, AND JANE A. REID

The United States Geological Survey (USGS) is a federal agency that provides research and analysis concerning natural resources. In the following excerpt from a USGS fact sheet, the authors describe the National Tsunami Hazard Mitigation Program (NTHMP), a partnership of several states and government agencies that seeks to further scientific understanding of tsunami hazards and to develop plans to prepare U.S. coastal communities for future tsunamis. The authors recommend that the USGS provide more information to tsunami centers—including improved seismic data, inundation (flood) maps, and studies of previous tsunami deposits—in order to improve the accuracy and timeliness of tsunami warnings.

Population pressures in coastal areas of the Pacific Ocean and the Caribbean are resulting in unprecedented shoreline development, putting residents, tourists, and property at increased risk from giant sea waves, called tsunamis. Often incorrectly referred to as "tidal waves," tsunamis can be generated either by distant earthquakes or by local seismic events, submarine landslides, or volcanic eruptions. For ocean-crossing tsunamis, there is often sufficient time to evacuate distant coastal areas, but more timely and accurate real-time tsunami forecasts are needed to avoid costly false alarms. Local tsunamis generated

Eric L. Geist, Guy R. Gelfenbaum, Bruce E. Jaffe, and Jane A. Reid, "Helping Coastal Communities at Risk from Tsunamis," *U.S. Geological Survey Fact Sheet 150-00*, 2000.

by quakes on active seismic zones in Alaska, the Pacific Northwest, the Caribbean, California, and Hawaii can arrive at nearby shorelines in minutes. In these cases, only better scientific understanding, informed disaster planning, and public education will save lives in future tsunamis.

Protecting lives and property from tsunamis demands a clear understanding of how tsunamis are generated, the identification of likely areas at risk, and mitigation efforts based on public education. The National Tsunami Hazard Mitigation Program (NTHMP), a partnership of the States of Alaska, California, Hawaii, Oregon, and Washington and the Federal Emergency Management Agency, National Oceanic and Atmospheric Administration (NOAA), and U.S. Geological Survey (USGS), is currently preparing tsunami inundation maps and implementing mitigation plans for states bordering the Pacific Ocean. The NTHMP is also providing tsunami early warnings for these states by means of deep-ocean tsunami detectors and new seismic stations on land. The cooperation of Federal and state agencies in the NTHMP is furthering scientific understanding of tsunami hazards and facilitating the development of plans to prepare coastal communities to better survive future tsunamis.

The Mission of the USGS

The mission of the USGS includes understanding the geologic mechanisms, frequency, magnitude, and physical consequences of natural hazards. In recent years, the USGS has upgraded its seismic networks to provide NOAA's tsunami warning centers with detailed earthquake information to aid in timely notification of the public. The USGS and NOAA are currently providing real-time seismic and tsunami information to state offices of emergency services in Alaska, Washington, Oregon, California, and Hawaii.

To ensure that its efforts to reduce the risk from tsunamis are focused where they will be most effective, the USGS convened a two-day workshop in Seattle, Washington, in January 2000. This workshop was attended by scientists and managers from the USGS, NOAA, state agencies, and academia. Based on needs identified by the workshop participants, the following recommendations on the role of the USGS in tsunami research were made:

Seismic networks—It is important that, as advances in technology and science allow, the USGS continue to enhance and improve the quality and quantity of seismic data supplied to tsunami warning centers. The USGS should also determine the need for additional strong-motion seismic stations along U.S. coasts. Further, the USGS should continue to develop software that supports tsunami warnings for local earthquakes, particularly in Hawaii, Alaska, the Pacific Northwest, and the Caribbean.

Earthquake source characterization—To make possible more accurate warnings and hazard assessments, better characterizations of critical earthquake source parameters are needed. Modern methods of analyzing seismic data developed by the USGS can be used by tsunami warning centers in an overall effort to improve the accuracy and timeliness of tsunami warnings. Further research is also recommended into using rapid seismic inversion algorithms to estimate sea-floor displacement, an indicator of likely tsunami size, which could be automated as part of local tsunami warning systems.

Hazard assessments—The NTHMP is coordinating the preparation of tsunami inundation maps for high-risk coastal communities in Alaska, California, Hawaii, Oregon, and Washington. The USGS can provide valuable guidance in the preparation of these maps by analyzing and interpreting deposits from historic and prehistoric tsunamis to estimate inundation limits, flow velocities, and recurrence intervals.

Coastal bathymetry [ocean water depth] and topography—Producing reliable and useful inundation maps for hazard assessment partially depends on accurate knowledge of the bathymetry and topography of coastal regions. The USGS, along with NOAA, NASA, and the Army Corps of Engineers, have proven capability to survey coastal and nearshore bathymetry and topography using modern techniques. It is recommended that the USGS coordinate with other Federal agencies to provide such information for hazard mitigation planning in high-priority areas of the Pacific Northwest, Alaska, Hawaii, California, and the Caribbean.

Sedimentary deposits as keys to tsunami character—Identification and interpretation of sedimentary deposits left behind by prehistoric tsunamis will improve our ability to assess the magnitude of tsunami risk in areas with an insufficient historical record. The USGS will provide expertise and leadership in sediment transport modeling to increase understanding of the mechanics of sediment transport in tsunamis and of the deposits they leave behind. Research would occur in field settings by integrating predictive modeling with laboratory and post-event studies.

Post-event rapid response—The visible effects of tsunamis are short-lived and may be lost after a single subsequent storm or during clean-up efforts employing earth-moving equipment. To determine the effects of tsunami inundation on land, the run-up elevation and distance, flow-speed and direction indicators, and patterns of sedimentary deposition must be mapped and quantified immediately following an event. USGS scientists should join the International Tsunami Survey Team, when warranted, to gather information about tsunami deposits and to calibrate sediment transport models.

Tsunamis generated by landslides and volcanic events—Landslides and volcano flank failures in coastal and island settings have also initiated large tsunamis. The accumulated knowledge of USGS scientists about submarine and coastal landslides and active volcanic processes should be focused on improving understanding of how and where these catastrophic mass failures may occur. This information then can be used in regional hazard assessments by Federal, state, and local authorities.

The efforts of USGS and other cooperators in the NTHMP are leading to a better understanding of tsunamis and how coastal populations can be prepared to survive their onslaught. The work of USGS scientists in tsunami research is only part of the ongoing efforts of the USGS to protect people's lives and property from geologic and environmental hazards in the coastal zones of the United States.

The Pacific Tsunami Warning Center

By Edward Bryant

Any submarine earthquake in the Pacific Ocean region can have oceanwide effects. As a result, Edward Bryant explains, the Pacific Tsunami Warning Center (PTWC) was developed for this area where the most devastating tsunamis occur. This warning system relies on the detection of earthquakes with a magnitude of 6.5 or greater on the Richter scale because these earthquakes may generate large tsunamis. The PTWC issues warnings to participating countries and, in addition, has extended its operations to include the International Tsunami Information Center (ITIC), which gathers and disseminates general information about tsunamis, fosters tsunami research, and conducts workshops on tsunami disaster education and preparedness. The PTWC, considered one of the most successful disaster mitigation programs in the world, reduces the risk that Pacific Ocean countries will suffer loss of life from long distance tsunamis.

Edward Bryant, a physical geographer and an associate professor of geoscience, researches climatic and oceanographic natural disasters and has received international recognition for his work on catastrophic tsunamis.

The most devastating oceanwide tsunami of the past two centuries have occurred in the Pacific Ocean. For that reason, tsunami warning is best developed in this region. Surprisingly, a coherent Pacific-wide warning system was only introduced following the Chilean tsunami of 1960. To date that system still has flaws. . . . The lead time for warnings in the Pacific is the best of any ocean, anywhere up to 24 hours depending upon the location of sites relative to an earthquake epicentre.

Following the Alaskan tsunami of 1946, the U.S. government established tsunami warning in the Pacific Ocean under the auspices of the Seismic Sea Wave Warning System. In 1948, this system evolved into the Pacific Tsunami Warning Center (PTWC). Warnings were initially issued for the United States and Hawaiian areas, but following the 1960 Chilean earthquake, the scheme was extended to all countries bordering the Pacific Ocean. Japan up until 1960 had its own warning network, believing at the time that all tsunami affecting Japan originated locally. The 1960 Chilean tsunami proved that any submarine earthquake in the Pacific Ocean region could spread oceanwide. The Pacific Warning System was significantly tested following the Alaskan earthquake of 1964. Within 46 minutes of that earthquake, a Pacific-wide tsunami warning was issued. This earthquake also precipitated the need for an International Tsunami Warning System (ITWS) for the Pacific that was established by the Intergovernmental Oceanographic Commission (IOC) of UNESCO at Ewa Beach, Oahu, Hawaii, in 1965. At the same time, other UNESCO/IOC member countries integrated their existing facilities and communications into the system. The United States National Weather Service currently maintains the Center. As of 1999, twenty-five countries cooperate in the Pacific Tsunami Warning System, in one of the most successful disaster mitigation programs in existence. These countries include Canada, the United States and its dependencies, Mexico, Guatemala, Nicaragua, Colombia, Ecuador, Peru, Chile, Tahiti, Cook Island, Western Samoa, Fiji, New Caledonia, New Zealand, Australia, Indonesia, Philippines, Hong Kong, Peoples Republic of China, Taiwan, Democratic Peoples Republic of Korea, Republic of Korea, Japan, and the Russian Federation. An additional ten countries or dependencies receive PTWC warnings. Many of the primary countries also operate national tsunami warning centres, providing warning services for their local area.

The Objectives of the International Tsunami Warning System

The objective of the International Tsunami Warning System is to detect, locate, and determine the magnitude of potentially tsunamigenic earthquakes occurring in the Pacific Basin or its immediate margins. The warning system relies on the detection of any earthquake 6.5 or greater on the Richter scale registering on one of thirty-one seismographs. . . . These stations are operated by the Center itself, the Alaskan Tsunami Warning Center, the United States Geological Survey's National Earthquake Information Center, and various international agencies. Once a suspect earthquake has been detected, information is relayed to Honolulu, where requests for fluctuations in sea level on tide gauges are issued to member countries operating sixty tide gauges scattered throughout the Pacific. These gauges can be polled in real time so that warnings can be distributed to a hundred dissemination points with three hours' advance notice of the arrival of a tsunami. The warnings are distributed to local, state, national, and international centres for any earthquake with a surface magnitude, M_S, of 7 or larger. A watch may also be disseminated by the International Tsunami Information Center (ITIC) at Ewa Beach for potential regional tsunami earthquakes with surface magnitudes, M_S, of less than 7.5. Administrators, in turn, disseminate this information to the public, generally over commercial radio and television channels. The National Oceanic and Atmospheric Administration (NOAA) Weather Radio system provides direct broadcast of tsunami information to the public via VHF transmission. The U.S. Coast Guard also broadcasts urgent marine warnings on medium frequency (MF) and very high frequency (VHF) marine radios. Anyone can also receive these tsunami warnings direct via e-mail by subscribing to the PTWC listserver at TSUNAMI@ITIC.NOAA.GOV. Local authorities and emergency managers are responsible for formulating and executing evacuation plans for areas under a tsunami warning. If no tsunami of significance is detected at tide gauges closest to the epicentre, the ITIC issues a cancellation. Once a significant tsunami has been detected, its path is then monitored to obtain information on wave periods and heights. These data are then used to define travel paths. . . .

Other Jobs of the ITIC

The ITIC also gathers and disseminates general information about tsunami, provides technical advice on the equipment required for an effective warning system, checks existing systems to ensure that they are up to standard, aids the establishment of national warning systems, fosters tsunami research, and conducts postdisaster surveys for the purpose of documentation and understanding of tsunami disasters. As part of its research mandate, the ITIC maintains a complete library of publications and a database related to tsunami. Research also involves the construction of mathematical models of tsunami travel times, height information, and extent of expected inundation for any coast. Planners and policy makers use results from these models to assess risk and to establish criteria for evacuation. The ITIC trains scientists of member states who, upon returning to their respective countries, train and educate others on tsunami programs and procedures, thus ensuring the continuity and success of the program. The Center also organises and conducts scientific workshops and educational seminars aimed towards tsunami disaster education and preparedness. In recent years, emphasis has been placed on the preparation of educational materials such as textbooks for children, instruction manuals for teachers, and videos for the lay public. Finally, the ITIC publishes an information and education newsletter on a regular basis. This newsletter is distributed to interested individuals, scientists, and institutions in approximately seventy countries.

Keeping the System Updated

The Pacific Warning Tsunami System is being updated to ensure that false alarms are not issued, and that all tsunami are detected. Satellite communications now speed up data collation and warning broadcasts. Other methods of detection are being investigated, including the positioning of sensitive pressure detectors on the ocean bottom adjacent to remote regions such as Alaska and Chile, where the highest-magnitude earthquake-induced tsunami originate. Shorter-period ocean swell will not be detected at these depths, but longer-period tsunami will. Today there is little chance that areas surrounding the Pacific Ocean should suffer loss of life from teleseismic [having long distance effects] tsunami. As of 1999, about three or four warnings a year are issued for the Pacific Ocean region. In the majority of cases, no tsunami ever eventuates; however, the fact remains that every country in the Pacific Ocean region—even ones not affected by past tsunami events—must always take these warnings seriously.

Tsunami Prediction and Mitigation

By Ellen J. Prager

In the following selection, Ellen J. Prager explains that tsunamis are difficult to predict reliably because their prediction is based on two variables: when the earthquakes that usually cause them will occur and whether or not the earthquakes will produce tsunamis. In addition, tsunamis are relatively rare events and have been recorded only recently. Consequently, scientists do not have much information on which to base predictions. The difficulty of predicting tsunamis makes advance planning and education especially important. Local communities must prepare themselves and know the warning signs of tsunamis in order for tsunami warning systems to be effective and for evacuation plans to be implemented. Tsunami warning systems have been established to alert coastal populations of potentially dangerous waves, but the warnings have often been false alarms. As a result, scientists are developing sensors called bottom-pressure recorders to detect tsunamis passing in the water, making short-term tsunami predictions more accurate.

Ellen J. Prager is a scientist who formerly worked with the United States Geological Survey and the National Geographic Society. She specializes in bringing an understanding of earth and marine science to the general public.

I n [recent] years there have been ten major tsunami events (Nicaragua, 1992; Flores, 1992; Okushiri, 1993; East Java, 1994; Mindoro, 1994; Kuril Islands, Russia, 1994; Manzanillo, 1995; Irian Jaya, Indonesia, 1996; Peru, 1996; and Papua New Guinea, 1998). In response to each, an international team of tsunami experts has been sent to the scene to gather information and learn as much as possible in the tsunami's aftermath. The purpose of the team is to collect data that will lead to a better understanding of tsunamis and ultimately save lives through improved hazard and risk assessment, education, prediction, and warnings. Much of what we know today about tsunamis comes directly from observations or eyewitness accounts immediately following an event. But scientists must act quickly, or valuable information may be lost because of cleanup activities and subsequent storms.

At each site, the International Survey Team works closely with local officials and disaster relief efforts to survey the aftermath of the tsunami, taking particular care to document evidence of how high, far, and fast the water flowed. Marks on walls and windows left by dirty flowing water are used to document the run-up height, a measure of how high the water reached. The run-up distance, the extent of the tsunami's penetration inland, is judged based on evidence such as the boundary of debris and where vegetation has been killed by saltwater. Every mark used as a basis for run-up estimates is photographed and precisely located using the Global Positioning System (GPS). Eyewitness accounts also provide invaluable information on the characteristics of a tsunami and the details of the wave right before it struck. Scientists compare the observations made by the team with computer simulations and attempt to model the height and speed of the tsunami as it approached and struck land, as well as the distance it traveled inland. In practical terms, experts hope that modeling can help tell people how far and how high they might need to run to escape an approaching tsunami in future events. The data collected by the International Tsunami Team in Papua New Guinea and elsewhere is beginning to reveal much about the science and nature of tsunamis. . . .

Difficulty in Predicting Tsunamis

If reliably predicting earthquakes is difficult, then reliably predicting tsunamis is nearly impossible. The prediction of both earthquakes and volcanic eruptions is generally based on probabilities, which in turn are based mainly on how often such events have happened in the past. For tsunamis, this sort of probability prediction is even more difficult. Not only do we need to know the probability of a given fault rupturing, but also whether it will produce a tsunami during a particular event. And tsunamis are much rarer phenomena than earthquakes. On a global scale, a magnitude 6 earthquake or larger occurs at least once every week. A comparatively large tsunami was, for many years, thought to occur only once every decade. Since 1992 there have been ten large tsunamis, but even so, based on the 1992–1998 period, a large tsunami could be predicted to occur only once every five months or so. Not only do tsunamis occur relatively infrequently, but their historic record is both short and incomplete.

Even in Japan, where tsunami documentation extends back 1,000 years, it is extremely difficult to predict the likelihood of a tsunami based on the available records. Tsunami descriptions contain varying amounts of detail, and it is only in the last 100 years that accurate wave records exist and have been correlated to specific earthquake events. Also, the landmarks referenced in reports have often changed or are now nonexistent. It is difficult to interpret a historic report that documents a tsunami's flooding relative to the house of a prominent citizen when that house (and citizen) no longer exists. The local conditions along the coast can also change. In effect, many of the past estimates of coastal inundation are meaningless, except for providing a record that an event did occur and a qualitative estimate of its size. Nonetheless, records and local lore enable residents to infer how often a tsunami is likely to occur. As in assessing earthquake risk and building quake-resistant structures, tsunami records are useful mainly to convince people of the hazards and to find ways of reducing the risks.

Probability of Tsunamis Following Earthquakes

What scientists do know is that a certain class of faults will invariably generate tsunamis if the rupture area during an earthquake is large enough. Where earthquakes have previously produced tsunamis, particularly on thrust faults within a subduction zone, they will probably do so again. Before the 1994 Mindoro, Philippines, earthquake, strike-slip faults were not supposed to trigger tsunamis, yet here a fairly moderate strike-slip event generated a sizable tsunami. And before 1998, earthquakes with relatively small to moderate moment magnitudes were considered unlikely to generate tsunamis, yet Papua New Guinea was hammered by a 15-meter wave after a small-to-moderate earthquake. Far less is known about the probabilities of tsunami-triggering mass movements, such as submarine landslides, being generated by an earthquake. Even in the densely populated coastal regions of the United States, landslide hazards have only recently been recognized. A map of the sea floor off Santa Monica Bay recently released by the U.S. Geological Survey reveals evidence that in the past large mass movements have occurred in the bay, suggesting that they may well happen again in the future.

Nonetheless, if we know the probability of a given fault rupturing, it is possible to estimate the likelihood for a tsunami and where and how it will strike. However, at any one locale, we must estimate the probability of all possible events, considering all faults within the area, and all segments of all faults. This process is incredibly time-consuming, for each computer simulation takes hours, and thousands of runs are needed. In the end, the final inundation or strike probability is only as accurate as the earthquake probability. Consequently, evacuation planning tends to rely more on the highest possible wave that may strike a given area, versus the probabilities of all potential events. Because the record of tsunami events is relatively short, it remains difficult to predict the likelihood of a tsunami in any one region. . . .

Reducing the Risks of Tsunamis

Tsunamis present a clear and deadly threat to coastal populations, particularly around the rim of the Pacific Ocean. Japan and Russia both have a long history of tsunami impacts. In the United States, Alaska, California, and Hawaii have been well recognized as areas at risk for tsunamis. Recent evidence suggests tsunami hazards also exist in the Caribbean and along the shores of the Gulf of Mexico, and are of particular concern in the Pacific Northwest. We cannot stop tsunamis from occurring any more than we can prevent volcanic eruptions and earthquakes, but we can try to reduce the risk to those living in harm's way.

To reduce risks, several aspects of tsunamis must be considered: the shortness or absence of a warning, a potentially long duration, and the extent and force of flooding in any given region. Ground shaking, a loud bang, or a rapid drop in sea level may precede a tsunami, or it may strike without precursory signs. Tsunamis may also pose a threat for a dangerously long time during events. Earthquakes can be devastating, but once the mainshock is over, the subsequent aftershocks tend to be weaker, so search and rescue efforts start immediately. Tsunamis generated within 80 to 160 kilometers from shore can strike in less than an hour, but additional waves can arrive much later. And when a tsunami enters a bay, it will likely set up water motions or oscillations that can last for days. The tsunami generated from the eruption of the Krakatau volcano in 1883 set the global ocean in motion for several days; related waves were recorded at Greenwich Observatory in England for a week after the actual event. Following a tsunami impact, it is often difficult for search-and-rescue personnel to plan their missions, for it is impossible to know whether or when a second or third wave is going to crash down. It is for this reason that advance planning and education is so important for any place that faces a risk of tsunamis. . . .

Tsunami Warning Systems

Tsunami warning systems are designed to alert coastal populations that a potentially disastrous series of monster waves is approaching. Ultimately, a tsunami warning system would operate and provide information in a way similar to the now-familiar and very effective system for hurricane warnings. There are four major tsunami warning centers in the Pacific: the Alaskan Tsunami

Smashed against cliffs or carried far inland and beached, ships close to the coastline are pummeled by tsunamis.

Warning Center near Anchorage, the Pacific Tsunami Warning Center near Honolulu, the French Polynesia Warning Center in Papeete, and the Japanese network in Japan. The Russians also operate a warning center on the eastern coast of Siberia, although this particular system is not always operational. At present, early warning centers are only capable of issuing a timely alert for distant tsunamis. A more modest system specifically designed for local tsunamis operates in Chile with technology provided by NOAA. By and large, however, locally derived tsunamis leave little time for detection or warning, partially because of our inability to detect tsunamis in the open ocean; however, this situation is starting to change.

Warning centers have traditionally issued alerts based on potential tsunami–generating earthquakes and historical data. Seismic stations throughout the world constantly transmit earthquake data to the regional tsunami warning centers. At the centers, the likelihood of tsunami formation is then assessed based on the location and magnitude of earthquakes, and in some instances the past history of tsunami generation in the area. If a tsunami is deemed likely, a warning is issued for coastal areas that could be effected within several hours or less, and a watch is issued for regions that may be impacted later. At the Alaska Tsunami Warning Center, regional warnings are issued within fifteen minutes of an earthquake and are based solely on seismic data. Any coastal earthquake over magnitude 7.0 results in an immediate tsunami warning. Warnings outside the Alaska Center's region are coordinated with the Pacific Tsunami Warning Center in Hawaii. There, a warning is issued based on seismic data combined with historical records and data from coastal tide-gauge stations.

Problems with False Alarms

With this warning system, there is no way to confirm tsunami predictions, and this has resulted in numerous false alarms. Unfortunately, false alarms can cost millions of dollars and, as in the story of the boy who cried wolf, erode the public's trust in those issuing the warnings. Since 1948, twenty tsunami warnings and evacuations have been carried out in Hawaii. Of the twenty warnings, fifteen were considered false alarms. For instance, during the magnitude 8.0 Kuril Island earthquake in 1993, a 10-meter tsunami slammed into and devastated the southern coast of Shitokan Island, north of Japan. Because the area lies adjacent to a subduction zone deep underwater, it is notorious for generating large tsunamis. So the Pacific Tsunami Warning Center issued an evacuation warning for the Hawaiian Islands three hours before the waves were estimated to arrive. Fortunately, when the waves arrived, they were less than 0.3 meter (1 foot) high. However, conservative estimates indicate that the false alarm and evacuation cost the Hawaiian economy roughly $30 million. But the costs of not evacuating or returning to an evacuated area too soon are clearly much greater. The tsunami triggered by the 1964 Good Friday earthquake in Alaska killed 159 people in Hawaii. In contrast, in the town of Crescent City, California, an evacuation order was issued before the first wave arrived, and many lives were saved. Unfortunately, some people returned to the evacuated area too soon, and eleven people perished due to late-arriving waves.

New Tsunami Sensors

To combat the problem of false alarms, confirm tsunami warnings, and possibly alert populations to the threat of locally triggered events, new technology is being developed at NOAA's Pacific Marine Environmental Laboratory. A new subsurface sensor has been designed to measure the pressure changes and timing associated with the passage of overlying waves, and to detect the specific characteristics indicative of a passing tsunami. Once a tsunami is detected, a surface buoy is triggered to send a signal via satellite to a shore-based warning center. When operational, these sensors will be able to confirm if a tsunami has actually formed and may provide a means of detecting locally derived events.

The new sensors are called bottom-pressure recorders, or BPRs. As a tsunami passes over the recorder (sitting on the sea floor), it measures the hydrostatic pressure changes associated with the passage of wave peaks and troughs. To detect a tsunami, it must measure pressure changes that are very small, but BPRs can record a 4-millimeter wave at a depth of 4,000 meters, equivalent to detecting a change of one part in a million—a truly impressive engineering achievement. Current work is focused on the difficult task of distinguishing tsunamis from wind waves and tides in the open ocean. Obviously, not every 1-meter-high wave in the open ocean is cause for concern, so the signals have to be carefully analyzed. Because a tsunami has such a long wavelength, the entire wave must go by before the data can be interpreted. This is not a problem when detecting a tsunami far offshore, but it is a great problem for one triggered and detected closer to the coast.

The wavelength of a tsunami is, in a sense, its most stealthy feature, for it also makes it invisible to satellite technology. Instruments aboard the TOPEX/POSEIDON satellite can detect wind waves on the surface of the ocean, but because the steepness of tsunamis is so small, they cannot "see" a tsunami. Wave steepness refers to the ratio of its height to its wavelength, and for a tsunami this is on the order of 1 to 10,000 or even smaller. Even if satellite detection was possible, a tsunami's racing speed adds to its stealthiness: an orbiting satellite would have to be in just the right place at just the right time to actually detect a tsunami.

The Ultimate Tsunami Warning System

In all respects, it seems that the new sea-floor pressure sensors offer the best hope for better and more reliable early warning systems. One had been deployed and was in operation for ninety days before being vandalized by fishermen. It is being replaced, and another four sensors are in the works. For effective warning, a much larger array of sensors is needed throughout the Pacific and off coastal areas at high risk. Eventually, the ultimate tsunami warning system will include a means to identify potential triggering events and detect or confirm tsunamis in the open ocean. Furthermore, each system will be linked to state-of-the-art tsunami models to predict where a tsunami will strike and the extent and force of coastal flooding expected, thus helping to determine where evacuations should take place. Some of these features are already in place, and others are under development.

Broadcasting the Tsunami Warnings

When a tsunami is expected or has been detected, the Tsunami Centers issue a warning or watch, depending on how much time there is before the impact is expected. Warning messages are transmitted to the appropriate authorities and the public over the National Warning System teletype system and over commercial radio and television broadcasts. The NOAA Weather Radio system and the U.S. Coast Guard broadcast tsunami information directly to the public. Information on tsunamis is also now available via email and the Internet. Evacuation plans and orders are issued by local and regional authorities. The warning system is designed so that evacuees should only return to low-lying areas once the "all clear" is announced and the threat of tsunamis has passed.

The Importance of Public Awareness

For the tsunami warning system to be effective, local communities must be educated and prepared. Some tourism and financial corporations plan and educate employees about tsunamis. And in some areas, such as the Pacific Northwest, school children and the public are being instructed on where to go should an alert be issued. As described earlier, inundation mapping is providing crucial information for education and preparation for tsunami hazards. . . . At a minimum, people who live within the coastal zone should be aware of potential tsunami precursors or warning signs. An earthquake or a noticeable and rapid retreat of the sea should inspire those along the coast to move fast and far from shore and, if possible, up. And although false alarms are bound to occur, those who choose to reside in or visit tsunami-prone areas should never become complacent about tsunami warnings. History has illustrated all too well the tragic impact of tsunamis in regions ill prepared for this demonstration of the Earth's fury. And as one expert says, when it comes to tsunamis, we should learn to expect the unexpected.

Tsunami Warning Systems

By Robert Koenig

Following the 1998 Papua New Guinea tsunami, which killed more than 2,100 people, scientists spent three years intensely studying the details of what was the decade's most devastating tsunami. Although scientists did not agree on the exact cause of the tsunami—whether it was generated by an earthquake or an underwater landslide—the study produced sophisticated seabed imaging and computer modeling techniques for studying tsunami generation. Despite these developments, Robert Koenig explains, some researchers emphasized the importance of collecting more data well in advance of a tsunami strike. This concern led to the creation of a coastal warning and deep-sea tsunami data collecting system called the Deep-Ocean Assessment and Reporting of Tsunamis (DART). This system consists of tsunami-detecting devices placed in strategic areas around the Pacific to pick up signs of tsunamis and relay these messages via satellite to ground stations. In addition to the DART system, a worldwide program has been proposed. Although scientists fear these systems may be powerless in the face of "megatsunamis," they continue to hope for improvement in warning times and preparations for tsunamis. Robert Koenig is a writer and correspondent for Science *magazine.*

When a colossal wave smashed into a spit of land along Papua New Guinea's coast on 17 July 1998, it destroyed three villages and killed more than 2100 people. That's when Costas Synolakis swung into action. The University of Southern California (USC) coastal engineer rushed to the site with an international team of tsunami scientists, including geologists, a seismologist, hydraulic engineers, and computer modelers, to find out every detail they could about the decade's most deadly tsunami. They measured marks left by the

Robert Koenig, "Researchers Target Deadly Tsunamis," *Science*, vol. 293, August 2001, p. 1,251. Copyright © 2001 by the American Association for the Advancement of Science. Reproduced by permission.

waves, surveyed damage, took statements from shaken survivors, and scrutinized seismologic and hydroacoustic data. But the evidence left them with a persistent puzzle: How could a moderate earthquake off the coast generate such a devastating tsunami, with 20-meter-high waves that impaled bodies on tree branches and smashed every structure in the 25-kilometer-long sand spit between the Pacific Ocean and the Sissano lagoon?

Three years of data collection, debate, and computer modeling may have turned up an answer. At recent tsunami conferences in Istanbul and Seattle, and in an article being prepared for publication [in the] fall of [2001] in the *Proceedings of the Royal Society*, Synolakis, seismologist Emile Okal of Northwestern University in Evanston, Illinois, and several colleagues propose what they believe to be the culprit: an underwater landslide. Evidence of such a "slump" lined up in a detailed bathymetry survey, or map of the ocean floor, co-sponsored by the Japan Marine Science and Technology Center and the South Pacific Applied Geoscience Commission. The survey showed sea-bottom scars of a major slump about 25 kilometers offshore of the Sissano lagoon. Studying seismologic and hydroacoustic data from the day of the tsunami, Okal concluded that the quake caused the slump, which in turn unleashed the deadly tsunami. And Synolakis and others on the survey team developed a computer model of the area that, they contend, confirms that such a "massive slump" offshore could have caused the Sissano tsunami. "This is the strongest evidence yet that 'local' tsunamis"—killer waves that originate just a few miles offshore of the site—"can be generated by massive underwater landslides," Synolakis says.

A Watershed for Tsunami Research

Some researchers dispute Synolakis's interpretation, arguing that the Sissano wave was caused mainly by the quake. But even more important than finding the cause of the Papua New Guinea tsunami, everyone agrees, are the tools developed in the search—including more sophisticated seabed imaging and computer models for tsunami generation and inundation. Marine geologist David Tappin of the British Geological Survey (BGS) calls the 3 years of ocean expeditions and scientific debates that followed the Papua New Guinea event "a watershed for tsunami research." According to Tappin, the "unprecedented depth of research" into the Sissano tsunami may allow researchers to "better understand why some areas are tsunami-prone and even to consider estimating the magnitude of the risk."

Despite those advances in bathymetry and computer modeling, other researchers argue that the most crucial challenge to tsunami research lies in gathering real-time data about killer waves before they near the shore. By spotting a tsunami early and taking its measure, proponents of such research say, scientists can help head off disaster before it strikes. Such data are now being provided by the Deep-ocean Assessment and Reporting of Tsunamis (DART) warning system, scheduled to deploy its sixth instrument [in August 2001] to help predict and analyze the giant waves on the open ocean.

Harbor-Wave History

The relation between earthquakes and tsunamis has been known for more than 2000 years—ever since the Greek historian Thucydides connected an Aegean tsunami in 426 B.C. to the quake that preceded it. Nevertheless, modern tsunami science is in its infancy. Only during the past decade have hydraulic engineers and other scientists begun using computers to model the three-dimensional evolution of tsunamis and devising inundation maps and early-warning systems for them. "Tsunamis killed more than 4000 people during the 1990s, but we have surprisingly little data to help us analyze them," says Eddie Bernard, an oceanographer who heads the U.S. National Oceanic and Atmospheric Administration's (NOAA's) Pacific Marine Environmental Laboratory (PMEL), which developed the DART system.

Tsunami generation involves intricate interactions among earthquakes, landslides, and "sympathetic" vibrations between the quake and the ocean above it. The Japanese word tsunami means "harbor wave"—a reference to the giant waves' ability to penetrate the protected harbors along Japan's coast. Although sometimes inaccurately called "tidal waves," tsunamis are produced by sudden underwater disruptions—usually undersea earthquakes but also submarine landslides and, far less often, volcanic eruptions or meteorites that hit the ocean.

The typical tsunami begins as a series of waves in the deep ocean, where they are not particularly dangerous. Although the wave pulses can race through the deep sea at speeds exceeding 700 kilometers an hour, their energy is dispersed along a wavelength as much as 750 kilometers wide. So a tsunami wave on the

Scientists collect data from a buoy in the Pacific Ocean to better understand the nature of tsunamis and to improve early warning systems.

open sea may be just a few meters high, with a slope that's sometimes too gentle for big ships to notice. It's not until tsunamis enter shallow coastal waters that they get higher and more dangerous—often "shoaling," or squeezing together into narrow monster waves that can be as high as 10-story buildings.

Since 1990, 11 major tsunami events have struck coasts from Java to Chile, killing more than 4000 people and causing hundreds of millions of dollars in damage. In all, there were about 80 tsunamis during that decade, many of which caused little damage because they were small or struck undeveloped coastlines. The National Geophysical Data Center in Boulder, Colorado, estimated that more than 80% of the world's tsunamis appear to be generated by undersea earthquakes around the Pacific Rim, where colliding tectonic plates lead to an unusually high level of seismic activity. But Synolakis and others believe that some of those tsunamis—especially local tsunamis, which are generated just a few kilometers off the coasts they strike—may be caused mainly by offshore landslides that are shaken loose by local or more-distant quakes.

Predicting the Waves of the Future

Whatever causes tsunamis, the more important challenge, Bernard believes, is to devise systems that can detect newly generated tsunamis in the deep ocean, collect information about them, and transmit it in real time to warning stations that could then evacuate threatened coastal areas. To provide a coastal warning system and to collect data about deep-sea tsunamis, NOAA has been deploying the DART system—starting in the North Pacific, along the Alaska Subduction Zone, which is the most dangerous generator of tsunamis that tend to strike Hawaii and the U.S. West Coast. Each DART assembly consists of a tsunami-detecting "bottom-pressure recorder" device on the ocean floor, which sends acoustic signals through the water to a car-sized surface buoy. The buoy transmits the data via satellite to ground stations, which relay them to NOAA's PMEL lab and several tsunami warning stations—including stations in Alaska and Hawaii. The warning stations, as well as efforts to map the likely local impact of tsunamis at specific sites along the U.S. West Coast, are part of the U.S. National Tsunami Hazard Mitigation Program, which began in 1996.

So far, three DART instruments have been set up along the Alaska zone (near the Bering Strait), and two have been deployed closer to the Oregon coast, near the Cascadia Subduction Zone, which is thought to generate large tsunamis every few centuries. A sixth DART station is being deployed in the deep ocean off South America's coast—not far from the site of the 23 June [2001] quake that generated a major tsunami along Peru's south coast. Oceanographer Frank L. Gonzalez, who directs PMEL's tsunami mapping center, says the new DART station "will intercept tsunami waves traveling from generation zones in the South American Subduction Zone to Hawaii, Japan, and other Pacific Rim countries." Gonzalez says the new equatorial DART station "will certainly help the warning centers issue faster, more reliable alerts for tsunamis generated off South America."

In the future, Bernard says, he plans to harness new science and technology to hone DART's ability to detect earthquake-generated tsunamis and spread warnings in advance. Better coverage will also be needed, he says. Bernard and his PMEL colleagues have proposed a worldwide program, tentatively called TROIKA, to deploy similar instruments in other tsunami-vulnerable regions. Such regions include the South Pacific, the Atlantic Ocean off the coast of Portugal (a 1755 tsunami destroyed much of Lisbon, killing 60,000 people), the Aegean Sea, and perhaps the Sea of Marmara and the Black Sea.

The Next Wave of Killer Waves

Despite the promise of DART and other systems for analyzing and predicting tsunamis, some experts worry that future dangers may overwhelm any defenses scientists are likely to devise. Judging from new evidence about "megatsunamis" in the distant past, such as the wave that battered the islands of the ancient Minoan civilization about 3500 years ago, they warn that more-destructive waves eventually will strike heavily populated coastlines, with potentially devastating impact. Ground zero is the Pacific Rim, where a seismically active "ring of fire" extending from the Bering Strait to the South Pacific unleashes earthquakes that trigger tsunamis.

Aside from the traditionally tsunami-battered Pacific islands of Japan and Hawaii, one of the most vulnerable regions is the Southern California coast. Jose Borrero, a postdoctoral researcher at USC who has worked with Synolakis in analyzing the tsunami threat along the California coast, says that "Southern California's offshore geology makes it ripe for producing tsunamis. Even a small tsunami along that coast would have a large potential for damage." Another West Coast threat comes from the Cascadia Subduction Zone, off the coasts of Washington, Oregon, and Northern California. Recent analysis of sand layers deposited in the region by ancient tsunamis suggests that one part of the Cascadia zone may be nearing a tsunami-generating earthquake, perhaps during this century.

Researchers also see potential danger in smaller seas such as the Mediterranean, the Black Sea, and even the tiny Sea of Marmara south of Istanbul. For example, a tsunami hit the French coastal city of Nice in 1979, and a small tsunami struck Izmit, Turkey, after an earthquake there in 1999. Istanbul, a metropolis of 13 million that rises along the Sea of Marmara and the Bosporus strait, could well be affected by a Marmara tsunami. "There will be another earthquake in this region, and it is likely to occur offshore, in the Sea of Marmara—making a tsunami likely," says BGS's Tappin. Ahmet C. Yalciner, an ocean engineer at Turkey's Middle East Technical University and co-director of the recent NATO tsunami workshop, fears that "underwater landslides could be a very important factor" in worsening a potential tsunami if an earthquake shakes under the Sea of Marmara.

But Bernard and others hope that advances in tsunami observation and warning systems, although powerless to influence the course of the giant waves, will help reduce the danger to vulnerable coasts. "We now have the equivalent of seismometers in the tsunami world," says Bernard. "Once we have collected data from 100 tsunamis in the deep ocean, we may have the potential to understand these complex events."

Major Tsunamis

Date	Origin	Effects	Death toll
June 7, 1692	Puerto Rico Trench, Caribbean	Port Royal, Jamaica permanently submerged	2,000
November 1, 1755	Atlantic Ocean	Lisbon destroyed	60,000
August 8, 1868	Peru–Chile Trench	Ships washed several miles inland; town of Arica destroyed	10–15,000
August 27, 1883	Krakatau	Devastation in East Indies	36,000
June 15, 1896	Japan Trench	Swept the east coast of Japan, with waves of 100 ft. (30.5 m) at Yoshihimama	27,122
December 28, 1908	Sicily	East coast of Sicily, including Messina, and toe of Italy badly damaged	58,000 (including earthquake victims)
March 3, 1933	Japan Trench	9,000 houses and 8,000 ships destroyed in Sanriku district, Honshu	3,000
April 1, 1946	Aleutian Trench	Damage to Alaska and Hawaii	159
May 22, 1960	South-central Chile	Coinciding with a week of earthquakes; damage to Chile and Hawaii	1,500 (61 in Hawaii)
March 27, 1964	Anchorage, Alaska	Severe damage to south coast of Alaska	115
August 23, 1976	Celebes Sea	Southwest Philippines struck, devastating Alicia, Pagadian, Cotabato, and Davao	8,000
December 12, 1992	Flores Island, Indonesia	Damage to south-central Indonesia	1,000
July 17, 1998	Papua New Guinea	Villages of Warapu and Arop completely destroyed; 5,000 left homeless	2,000

GLOSSARY

amplitude: The maximum height of a wave crest or depth of a trough.

arrival time: The time of arrival, usually referring to the first wave of the tsunami at a particular location.

bathymetry: The science of measuring the depths of oceans, seas, and so forth.

bore: A traveling wave with an abrupt vertical front or wall of water. Under certain conditions, the leading edge of a tsunami wave may form a bore as it approaches and runs onshore. A bore may also be formed when a tsunami wave enters a river channel and may travel upstream, penetrating to a greater distance inland than the general inundation.

harbor resonance: The continued reflection and interference of waves from the edge of a harbor or narrow bay, which can cause amplification of the wave heights and extend the duration of wave activity from a tsunami.

inundate: To move in waves, to flood, or to cover with a flood.

inundation: The depth, relative to a stated reference level, to which a particular location is covered by water.

inundation area: An area that is flooded with water.

leading-depression wave: An initial tsunami wave that is a trough, causing a drawdown of the water level.

leading-positive wave: An initial tsunami wave that is a crest, causing a rise in water level; also called a leading-elevation wave.

local tsunami: A tsunami whose source is within one thousand kilometers of the area of interest; local, or near-field, tsunamis have a very short travel time (thirty minutes or less). *Local tsunami* is also sometimes used to refer to a tsunami of landslide origin.

long-period: A term used to identify a tsunami wave that has been generated by large sources, such as large earthquakes or falling meteors.

Ms (surface-wave magnitude): The magnitude of an earthquake as measured from the amplitude of seismic surface waves; often referred to by the media as "Richter" magnitude.

period: The length of time between two successive peaks or troughs; the time may vary due to complex interference of waves, but tsunami periods generally range from five to sixty minutes.

regional tsunami: A tsunami that has waves with travel times of thirty minutes to two hours; also called a midfield tsunami.

run-up: The maximum height of the water onshore observed above a reference sea level.

short-period: A term used to identify tsunami waves generated from smaller sources such as landslides and smaller earthquakes.

strike-slip earthquake: An earthquake caused by horizontal slip along a fault.

subduction zone: An elongated region along which a block of crusts descends relative to another crustal block.

swath mapping: A method of mapping the seafloor that covers large areas in very short periods of time, collecting continuous data.

teleseismic tsunami: A tsunami that affects long distances across an ocean.

teletsunami: A tsunami whose source is more than one thousand kilometers away from the area of interest; also called a distant-source or far-field tsunami.

thrust earthquake: An earthquake caused by slip along a gently sloping fault where the rock above the fault is pushed upward relative to the rock below; a thrust earthquake is the most common type of earthquake source of damaging tsunamis.

tidal wave: A common term for tsunami used in older literature, historical descriptions, and popular accounts. Tides, caused by the gravitational attractions of the sun and moon, may increase or decrease the impact of a tsunami but have nothing to do with a tsunami's generation or propagation.

travel time: The time (usually measured in hours and tenths of hours) it takes a tsunami to travel from its source to a particular location.

trough: The long, narrow depression between waves.

tsunami: A Japanese term derived from the characters *tsu* (meaning "harbor") and *nami* (meaning "wave"). *Tsunami* is now generally accepted by the international scientific community to describe a series of traveling waves in water produced by the displacement of the seafloor due to submarine earthquakes, volcanic eruptions, landslides, and meteors (on rare occasions).

tsunami earthquake: A tsunamigenic earthquake that produces a much larger tsunami than expected for its magnitude.

tsunamigenic earthquake: An earthquake that produces a measurable tsunami.

tsunami magnitude: A number that characterizes the strength of a tsunami based on the tsunami wave amplitudes. Several different tsunami magnitude dertermination methods have been proposed.

turbidity current: A dense current carrying clay, silt, and sand.

wavelength: The distance measured between one wave crest and another.

Measurements
1 mile = 5,280 feet = 1.6 kilometers
1 nautical mile = 6,076 feet = 1.85 kilometers
1 kilometer = 3,281 feet = 0.62 miles
1 meter = 3.28 feet

FOR FURTHER RESEARCH

Books

David Alexander, *Natural Disasters*. New York: Chapman and Hall, 1993.

Melvin Berger, *Disastrous Floods and Tidal Waves*. New York: Franklin Watts, 1981.

Edward Bryant, *Natural Hazards*. New York: Cambridge University Press, 1991.

David Chapman, *Natural Hazards*. New York: Oxford University Press, 1994.

James Cornell, *The Great International Disaster Book*. New York: Scribner's, 1976.

Dongal Dixon, *The Earth, Its Wonders, Its Secrets: Natural Disasters*. Pleasantville, NY: Reader's Digest, 1997.

Jon Erickson, *Quakes, Eruptions, and Other Geologic Cataclysms*. New York: Facts On File, 1994.

Robert H. Maybury, *Violent Forces of Nature*. Mt. Airy, MD: Lomond Publications, 1986.

Bill McGuire, Ian Mason, and Christopher Kilburn, *Natural Hazards and Environmental Change*. New York: Oxford University Press, 2002.

Mark Monmonier, *Cartographies of Danger*. Chicago: University of Chicago Press, 1997.

Douglas Myles, *The Great Waves*. New York: McGraw-Hill, 1985.

Lesley Newson, *Devastation! The World's Worst Natural Disasters*. New York: DK Publishing, 1998.

Andrew Robinson, *Earthshock: Hurricanes, Volcanoes, Earthquakes, Tornadoes, and Other Forces of Nature*. New York: Thames and Hudson, 2002.

Keith Smith, *Environmental Hazards: Assessing Risk and Reducing Disaster.* New York: Routledge, 2001.

Ted Steinberg, *Acts of God.* New York: Oxford University Press, 2000.

Jane Walker, *Tidal Waves and Flooding.* New York: Shooting Star Press, 1994.

Tony Waltham, *Catastrophe: The Violent Earth.* New York: Crown, 1978.

John Whittow, *Disasters.* Athens: University of Georgia Press, 1979.

Anders Wijkman and Lloyd Timberlake, *Natural Disasters.* Washington, DC: Earthscan, 1985.

Periodicals

Kathryn Brown, "Tsunami! At Lake Tahoe?" *Science News,* June 2000.

Kenneth Chang, "Experts Find Clues to Cause of Deadly Pacific Tsunami," *New York Times,* April 23, 2002.

David Chester, "The 1755 Lisbon Earthquake," *Progress in Physical Geography,* September 2001.

Michael Christie, "Nature's Coastal Hazards," *Gold Coast Bulletin,* March 2002.

Rene S. Ebersole, "The Wave of the Future," *Current Science,* November 2000.

Samuel Eugenie, "Wave Goodbye," *New Scientist,* September 2001.

Tim Folger, "Waves of Destruction," *Discover,* May 1994.

Beth Geiger, "Hawaii's Slip Is Showing," *Current Science,* May 2002.

Daryl Gray, "Monster Wave Alert," *Current Science,* April 2000.

Dan Hogan, "Tsunami Terror," *Current Science,* February 1998.

Robert Irion, "Tsunamis Threaten California," *Science Now,* December 2000.

Nicola Jones, "Get Ready for a Killer Wave," *New Scientist*, September 2002.

John S. MacNeil, "An Atlantic Tidal Wave," *U.S. News & World Report*, May 15, 2000.

Jane M. Matty, "Tsunamis," *Rocks and Minerals*, January 1999.

Norman Miller, "Making Shock Waves," *Geographical Magazine*, June 2000.

Richard Monastersky, "Waves of Death," *Science News*, October 1998.

Fred Pearce, "On Shaky Ground," *Geographical Magazine*, June 2002.

David Perlman, "Threat of Killer Waves," *San Francisco Chronicle*, September 10, 2001.

Charles W. Petit, "Wave Goodbye to Florida," *U.S. News & World Report*, September 10, 2001.

Lawrence Richter Quinn, "Rage of Waves," *Risk and Insurance*, September 2000.

Sarah Simpson, "Killer Waves on the East Coast?" *Scientific American*, October 2000.

Marshall Tristan, "The Drowning Wave," *New Scientist*, October 2000.

——, "Tsunamis a Threat to Pacific Northwest," *USA Today Magazine*, December 2001.

Gabrielle Walker, "Catch the Wave," *New Scientist*, December 2000.

Websites

Hawaii's School of Ocean and Earth Science and Technology, www.soest.hawaii.edu. This site has up-to-date information about tsunami hazards and predictions as well as news stories, an "Ask an Earth Scientist" section, and a weekly news bulletin.

Savage Earth: Waves of Destruction, www.pbs.org. This website features animated illustrations, articles on tsunamis, an "Ask the Experts" section, and photos of tsunamis.

Tsunami Reseach Program, www.pmel.noaa.gov. This program, sponsored by the National Oceanic and Atmospheric Administration, seeks to mitigate tsunami hazards to Hawaii, California, Washington, and Alaska. The website has information on the National Tsunami Hazard Mitigation Program as well as mapping efforts, events, and data on tsunamis.

Tsunamis and Earthquakes, http://walrus.wr.usgs.gov/tsunami. This USGS website provides general information on how local tsunamis are generated by earthquakes. It also includes animations, virtual-reality models of tsunamis, and summaries of past research studies.

Tsunamis Theme Page, www.cln.org. This website is a supplement to the study of tsunamis and provides links to other tsunami sites.

University of Southern California Tsunami Research Group, www.usc.edu. This group is dedicated to the investigation of tsunamis and is actively involved with all aspects of tsunami research, including hazard mitigation and planning. The website provides a world map that shows locations of past tsunamis, video animation with simulation and footage of tsunami activity, articles on tsunamis, and useful links.

Welcome to Tsunami! www.geophys.washington.edu. Sponsored by the University of Washington, this website has been developed to provide general information about tsunamis. It is an interactive site that includes information on recent tsunami events.

West Coast and Alaska Tsunami Warning Center, www.wcatwc.gov. This site explains the physics behind tsunamis and how they are generated and propagated. It also includes FAQs (frequently asked questions) and other tsunami links and references.

INDEX

Alaska, 20, 23, 46–47
Alaskan Tsunami Warning
  Center, 68, 69
Aleutian Islands, 46–47
Arica, Chile (1868), 25–26, 30–31,
  35
Atlantic Ocean, 18, 22–23

Bernard, Eddie, 75, 77, 79
Berninghausen, William, 33
Billings, L.G., 30–31, 36–37
Borrero, Jose, 78
bottom-pressure recorders, 15,
  70–71, 77
Bryant, Edward, 39, 60

Canary Islands, 22–24
Caribbean Sea, 18, 56
Chile, 25, 30–31, 35
  early warning system for, 32
  frequency of earthquakes and
    tsunamis in, 29
  instability of coastline of, 26–27
  1946 tsunami in, 47
  1960 earthquake in, 13–14
Coast Guard, U.S., 62, 71
coastlines
  instability of, in Peru and Chile,
    26–27
  population development along,
    23, 24, 56
  at risk for tsunamis, 67
  topography of
    early warning systems and
      knowledge of, 58

impact of waves and, 27
computer modeling, 14, 65
Cumbre Vieja volcano, 22–24

Day, Simon, 22, 23–24
Deep-Ocean Assessment and
  Reporting of Tsunamis
  (DART), 75, 77–78
detection
  bottom-pressure recorders and,
    15, 70–71, 77
  difficulties of, 13, 21, 46
  of earthquakes, 61–62
  precursory signs of tsunamis,
    27–28, 67
  satellites and, 63, 71
  seismic stations and, 57–58, 69
Drake, Dorothy, 42–43
Dudley, Walter C., 48

early warning systems
  basis of alerts from, 58–59,
    65–66, 69
  coastline topography and, 58
  failure of, during Papua New
    Guinea tsunami, 49
  false alarms and, 69–70
  in Japan, 69
  ocean-crossing tsunamis and, 56
  in Pacific Ocean, 60
  response time of, 32
  in Russia, 69
  see also detection; specific names of
    tsunami warning centers
earthquakes